Railways of Suffolk

By
Malcolm R. White

GENERAL INFORMATION

THIS PUBLICATION

Every effort has been made to ensure that information contained in this publication is accurate and for this reason many sources have been consulted. These include official documentation, local diaries, media and enthusiasts resources and numerous accredited research works. However, when considering such a complex historical subject with some details gathered from records that were provided by other parties in the distant past, 100% accuracy is difficult to guarantee. Books in this series are part of the National Published Archive and as such are included in the library collections of the British Library, the National Library of Scotland, the National Library of Wales, the Universities of Oxford and Cambridge, Trinity College, Dublin and, when appropriate, The National Museum of Science & Industry. The Suffolk county boundary existing in 2010 has been used throughout this book with regard to stations, yards and depot locations. This series is published on a non profit basis by an enthusiast for the enthusiast and not, as in the great majority of similar works, for financial gain of the author(s) and a commercial publisher. Any profit that does arise from the sale of books in this series is donated to charity and good causes.

PHOTOGRAPHIC OWNERSHIP AND COPYRIGHT

 The names of known photographers, copyright owners or originators are shown throughout the book in italics at the end of each photographic caption.

Note - In view of the current train operator's comprehensive rules and restrictions governing photography, no photographs taken on any of "their" stations are included in this book. At the time of writing this operator was National Express East Anglia.

ACKNOWLEDGEMENTS

Assisting either directly or indirectly in this publication have been the Anglian Rail Archive, Foxearth & District Local History Society, The Midland Railway Centre, Mr. Carl Baker, Mr. Ivan Bunn, Mr. Peter Calvert, Mr. Alan Calladine, Mr. John Chalcraft, Mr. Brian Chambers, Mr. David Chappell, Mr. Stanley Earl, Mr. Norman Fairhead, Mr. Alan G. Finch, Mr. Tim Heaps, Mr. Alfred Hubbard, Mr. Peter Killby, the late Mr. Malcolm Maclean, Mrs. Cathryn White, Mr. David White and Mr. Allan Wood. Sources of information consulted for this book are considerable and include the following :- Cambridgeshire Archives and Deeds [CCC 2009], Eastern Counties Railway Guide 1851[ECR], Railway Guide through England [Black 1857], Railway, Canal and Joint Stock Cases [Nicholl, Hare, Carron, Oliver and Beavan 1855], Road Book for Rail, Eastern (Western) Division [Sharpe 1855], Table of Local Acts (Office of Public Sector Information 2009), Railways of the United Kingdom [Scrivenor 1849], The Statutes of the United Kingdom and Ireland [Rickards 1861], Railway and other Steamers [Duckworth & Langmuir 1948], The Felixstowe Dock and Railway Company [FD&RC 1975] and minutes of various Parliamentary Committees and legal cases. Information was also derived from editions of the British Railways Eastern Region Magazine, The National Archive, Hansard, local history societies, news publications and magazines published by the Great Eastern Railway Society, Ipswich Transport Society, Mid Suffolk Light Railway Museum, Southwold Railway Trust and some on-line sources such as those provided by Stately Trains and the Deltic Preservation Society.

Special thanks to Mr. Ron White, the owner of Colour Rail during the time that this book was being written, for the specialised assistance he kindly provided. I am especially grateful to Mr. Richard Casserley for allowing the use of many of his photographs and those of his father, Mr. Henry C. Casserley, in this book.

Successful completion of *Railways of Suffolk* would not have been possible without the valuable help provided by Mr. Stuart Jones BA. Stuart has provided important editorial support for all titles in the series and has done so again with this book.

CAPTIONS

Front Cover (Main Photograph) - Class 37/7 Co-Co No. 37714 heads west from Bury St. Edmunds on Monday 16th July 1990 with a train loaded with scrap metal. Entering service in 1961 as No. D6724, this locomotive was renumbered 37024 in 1974 and 37714 in 1988. In 2001, No. 37714 went to Spain on hire and was initially renumbered L031 and later L23. *Copyright Malcolm R. White*

Front Cover (Small Photograph) - The scene at Haverhill on a summer evening as the setting sun catches the front of Class B1 4-6-0 No. 61171 stopped at the station whilst working a westbound express passenger train. *Copyright Malcolm R. White*

Title Page - One of Yarmouth South Town's Class B17/4 4-6-0 locomotives waits at Beccles with a train from London Liverpool Street on Monday 21st July 1952. This locomotive, No. 61664 *Liverpool,* was scrapped at Stratford in June 1960. *Copyright Mid Rail Trust, Ripley*

Opposite - Class 37/0 Co-Co No. 6744 passes Saxmundham Junction bound for Lowestoft with a weed killing train. Later renumbered 37044, this locomotive became Class 37/7 No. 37710 in 1988. It was withdrawn and stored in 2008. *Copyright Malcolm R. White - Photographer Dr. Ian C. Allen.*

CONTENTS

INTRODUCTION

The majority of the railways in Suffolk were established in the days of seemingly unstoppable expansion of the rail network. This rapid period of expansion was followed in the 20th century by a period of contraction and stabilisation lasting around 50 years, when many lines and stations, opened with high expectations, closed leaving local communities replying on road transport. These closures meant the disappearance of scenes where often elderly steam engines with carriages to match, or the new diesel multiple units, made their leisurely way between historic and attractive Suffolk villages and towns, often set in idyllic countryside. Whilst many folk may miss these wonderful nostalgic scenes, the running and infrastructure costs together with declining goods traffic and passenger numbers meant that closure was not unexpected when the "withdrawal of passenger service" notices were posted and the final trains ran. Having been born and lived in the county all my life, I was fortunate to sample some of these railway delights before it was decided by those in authority that closure was the only way forward. To justify the withdrawal of services from two of Suffolk's railway gems, British Railways revealed that the cost of running the railway between Sudbury and Haverhill, and that between Bury St. Edmunds and Long Melford, outweighed revenue by at least three to one. Another example was the often very busy cross border railway between Yarmouth and Lowestoft where expenditure was said to exceed revenue by four to one. The way in which this figure had been arrived at was not made public. Prior to closure this once important route had been reduced to a single track basic railway with no signals or manned stations. It was worked by a diesel multiple unit shuttling back and forth between the two towns.

Much has changed since the days when railway closures were considered normal practice and, at the time of writing, it is satisfying that many Suffolk towns and villages such as Beccles, Bury St. Edmunds, Darsham, Halesworth, Lowestoft, Oulton Broad, Saxmundham and Woodbridge have again direct services to the capital. More passengers are travelling than for many years, a major new railway served tourist attraction in Suffolk is proposed, new trains have been ordered and a vast expansion of freight generated in Suffolk and carried by rail is planned. In late 2009, it was proposed that a new line be laid between the East Suffolk line and the Norwich - Ipswich line at Ipswich, thereby allowing container traffic between Felixstowe, the Midlands and the North to bypass Ipswich station and the main line to London.

Despite these apparent positive indicators, in 2009 the train operator National Express East Anglia produced a consultative document containing proposals to withdraw through services to London in 2010 from two of Suffolk's important rail routes, and involving several towns in the county. In the consultative process that commenced in early 2010, the Labour Government backed these proposals.

The comprehensive railway heritage of Suffolk includes a unique narrow gauge railway, engineering depots and works, three rail served dock and port installations, small country village stations, busy inland and coastal town stations, slow pick up goods trains, major flows of rail borne containers, fast main line and slow country passenger services, ferries, marine services and pleasure steamers. With such a diverse and notable past, hopefully the industry is destined for an equally interesting future. The period covered by this book pictorially concludes in the 1990s, by which time the structure of the British Railways organisation was being broken up and parts sold off. A small number of more recent scenes showing steam locomotives in British Railways livery at work in the county have been included

This book is intended to complement the other local railway titles in this series, and in order to cater for the increasing numbers of those mainly interested in heritage diesel traction, the pictorial content features both steam and diesel motive power.

Malcolm White
Lowestoft
June 2010

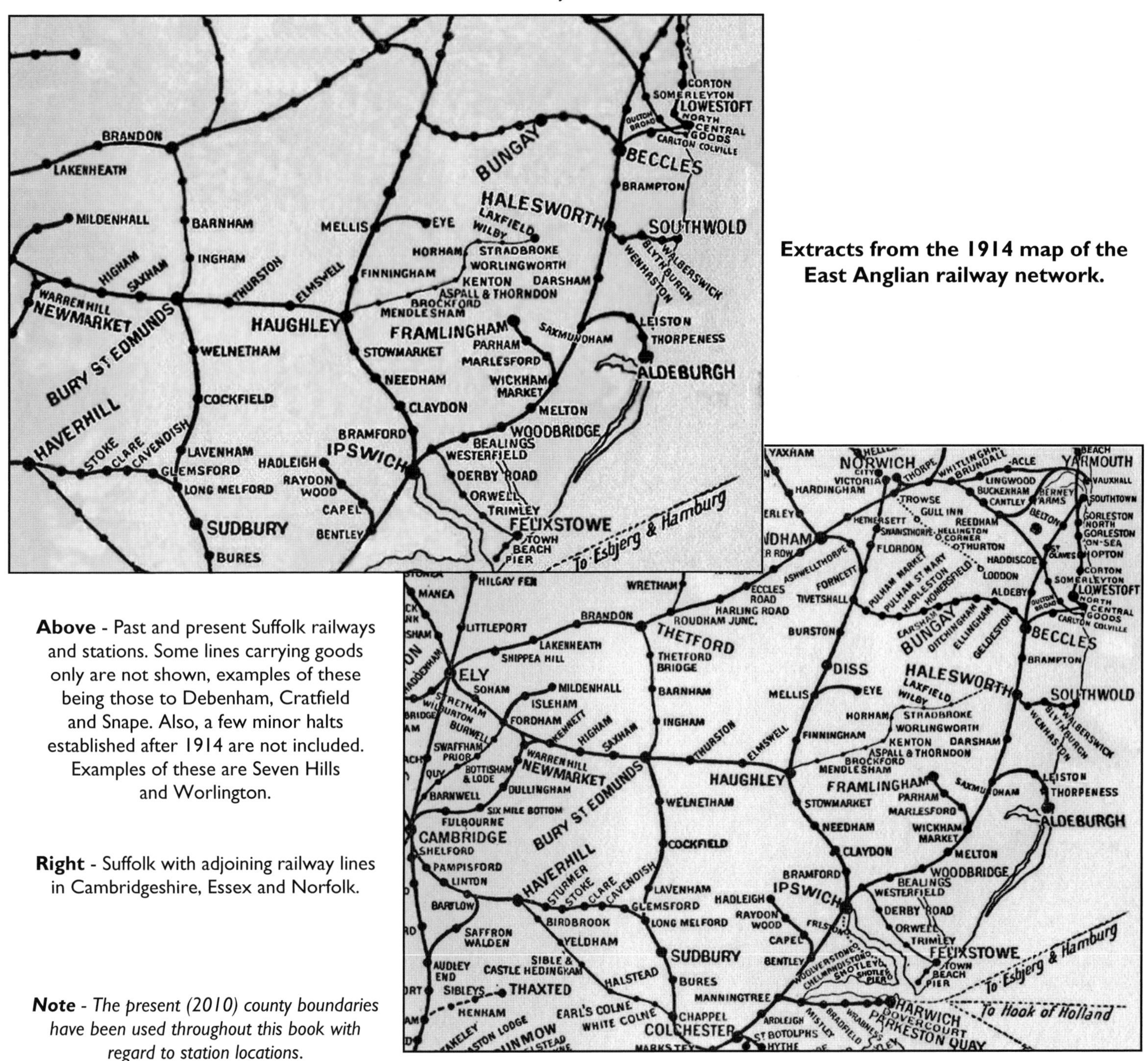

Extracts from the 1914 map of the East Anglian railway network.

Above - Past and present Suffolk railways and stations. Some lines carrying goods only are not shown, examples of these being those to Debenham, Cratfield and Snape. Also, a few minor halts established after 1914 are not included. Examples of these are Seven Hills and Worlington.

Right - Suffolk with adjoining railway lines in Cambridgeshire, Essex and Norfolk.

Note - *The present (2010) county boundaries have been used throughout this book with regard to station locations.*

BRIEF DESCRIPTION OF SUFFOLK RAILWAY STATIONS AND OTHER SITES

Notes relating to this section can be found on pages 31 and 32

Aldeburgh

Aldeburgh was the terminus of the 8¼ mile single track railway from Saxmundham and opened after the line had been extended from the original terminus at Leiston. The extension and station were built by the East Suffolk Railway (ESR) and opened on Thursday 12th April 1860; it was operated by the Eastern Counties Railway (ECR) from the outset. Aldeburgh was located 30½ miles from Ipswich and 99¼ miles from London Liverpool Street and in comparison to the size of the local population, the station seemed quite large. However it was hoped that the popularity of this seaside resort would increase and the station was built accordingly. Until Tuesday 1st June 1875, the station name was listed as Aldeborough or Aldborough. The terminus had a small brick built engine shed complete with servicing facilities. This closed before 1956 when diesel multiple units were introduced on the line and was a sub shed of Ipswich (32B). The fishing industry was an important user of the railway with locally caught fish being sent by rail to the wider market. Aldeburgh was closed to passengers by British Railways (BR) after the last train ran on Saturday 10th September 1966. Goods traffic was officially handled at Aldeburgh until Monday 30th November 1959 although some traffic may have been handled later than this. The station site is now occupied by housing and a road junction.

Aspall & Thorndon (Mid Suffolk Light Railway)

Set in an area renowned for cider making, Aspall & Thorndon was an intermediate station on the light railway that ran between Haughley and Laxfield. The station was located 8½ miles from Haughley and 10½ miles from Laxfield. Aspall & Thorndon opened to goods traffic on Tuesday 20th September 1904 and to passengers on Tuesday 29th September 1908. The station buildings were of the usual MSLR timber frame and corrugated iron construction. The last passenger train ran on Saturday 26th July 1952 after which the line was closed by BR. Prior to closure, the passenger service had been two trains per day in each direction. Aspall & Thorndon was noted in timetables as the station for the nearby village of Debenham. A large section of the platform still exists.

Barnby-Siding/Loop and Signal Box

Located between Carlton Colville (later Oulton Broad South) and Beccles, the siding at Barnby was used for transhipping items such as sugar beet, potatoes, livestock, coal, bricks and during World War II supplies for RAF Beccles. However, Barnby is renowned for the loss of life and injuries incurred in the serious accident that occurred at around 7.00pm on Christmas Eve 1891. With dense freezing fog drifting across from the marshes, the well filled 12.30 pm down train from London collided head on with the equally well filled 6.27pm up train from Lowestoft. Normal practice was that the up train should be held in Barnby siding loop waiting for the down train to pass on the single line but due to the appalling visibility the signals could not be seen and the down train from Beccles smashed into the up train from Lowestoft. Driver Borrett with the up train had immediately applied the Westinghouse brakes on the train when he made out the outline of the signal box but the train continued past the siding loop points slipping along on the ice covered rails, but it was too late, and despite the action of the driver of the down train in trying to stop when realising the danger, the collision occurred. There were three fatalities and over 30 people seriously injured. One of those killed was the fireman from the up train, 26 year old Henry John Read whose body, very badly scalded, was found in the tender of the locomotive he was firing. The others were Frederick Mallett, engine fitter, who was found dead by the side of the line and Mr. Lake, guard of the down train, who was on relief duty for another guard. His body was discovered dreadfully mutilated, in the compartment next to the engine. Immediately news of the collision was received, the GER ambulance team was transported to the scene by a special train hastily made up by Beccles Station Master J. W. Smith and headed by GER locomotive No. 28. This relief train took bandages, splints, and other urgently needed medical supplies to the scene and brought survivors back to the station where hundreds of people had assembled. Many local doctors and Beccles hospital staff were transported to the scene and some of the casualties were treated by medical staff at The Swan public house before going to hospital at Lowestoft or Beccles. It was stated at the time that it was a miracle that many more people had not been killed in view of the appalling circumstances. The grave of Fireman Read is in Lowestoft Cemetery and noted on the large tombstone is that it was paid for by the young man's work colleagues.

(Some information extracted from the East Suffolk Gazette report of the incident)

Barnham

Situated close to the Norfolk/Suffolk border, Barnham station was opened on Wednesday 1st March 1876 by the Bury St. Edmunds & Thetford Railway. It was closed to passengers by BR from Monday 8th June 1953 and to goods traffic from Monday 27th June 1960. This intermediate station was located 9¼ miles from Bury St. Edmunds and 3½ miles from Thetford on the Bury St. Edmunds Northgate - Thetford railway line. Due to the major military presence in the locality, the station and sidings were extremely busy in both World Wars. During World War II a short siding went to a high security military compound and into a loading shed at Little Heath. More recently it has emerged that a chemical and nuclear storage facility once existed nearby.

Bealings

Bealings was an intermediate station built by the EUR, opened with the ESR on Wednesday 1st June 1859, and operated by the ECR from that date. The station was on the Ipswich - Beccles - Yarmouth/Lowestoft railway line and situated 7¼ miles from Ipswich, 33¼ miles from Beccles and 76 miles from London Liverpool Street. Situated near the small village of Little Bealings, the station was closed to passengers by BR from Monday 17th September 1956 and to goods traffic from Monday 19th April 1965. Now in private ownership and in use as a business centre, the former goods shed and main station buildings are on the down side of the line. In addition to agricultural produce and coal, the station handled traffic for the nearby RFC/RAF Martlesham Heath aerodrome which opened in January 1917 and closed in April 1963.

Beccles

Beccles was once an important junction station with railway lines running north to Yarmouth South Town, east to Lowestoft, south to Ipswich and west to Tivetshall (for Norwich) via Bungay and Harleston. The passenger service to Tivetshall was withdrawn after the last train ran on Saturday 3rd January 1953, but this line was not immediately closed to goods traffic. The line to Yarmouth South Town closed to passengers after the last train ran on Sunday 1st November 1959. Prior to the withdrawal of these services it had been 19½ miles to Tivetshall and 12½ miles to Yarmouth South Town. Following the closure of the Yarmouth South Town line, Beccles became an intermediate station on the Ipswich - Lowestoft railway line being located 40½ miles from Ipswich, 8½ miles from Lowestoft Central, and 109¼ miles from London Liverpool Street.

The line through Beccles was opened by the ESR to passengers on Monday 4th December 1854 and to goods traffic early in 1855, having been built by the Halesworth, Beccles & Haddiscoe Railway. In its heyday, the infrastructure at Beccles included four platforms with a platform bridge between the island and down platforms, two signal boxes, an engine shed, turntable, locomotive servicing facilities, a large goods shed, many sidings and a rail connection to a nearby maltings. For much of the time, the engine shed was considered an outstation of Lowestoft. The first engine shed was a small single road structure situated south of the station and near Beccles South Signal Box. This was replaced in the late 1880s by a more substantial two road building north of the station and after many years of non railway use, this was demolished in March 2006 to make way for a warehouse and superstore. Following the introduction of radio signalling and general modernisation of the East Suffolk Line in the mid 1980s, the track through the station was reduced to a single line with one platform in use. To make way for redevelopment both the goods shed and the majority of the nearby rail connected maltings have been demolished in recent years. With the modernisation of the line, the island platform shelter and a footbridge were demolished. The remaining station buildings have not been in railway use for many years and a semi open bus-stop type shelter is provided for passengers' use. Beccles became unstaffed from Monday 6th March 1967 and closed to goods traffic from Wednesday 31st January 1968. At the time of writing (2010) the provision of a passing loop and the return to use of the island platform is being considered as part of the proposals to enhance the services between Lowestoft and Ipswich. Also, as part of the plans to regenerate the area around the station, a new car park near the north end of the present single platform is proposed for rail users.

Bentley / Bentley Junction

Bentley was once a junction station with railway lines running north east to Ipswich, south west to Colchester and London, and north west to the nearby town of Hadleigh. The station was opened by the EUR in June 1846, closed by BR to goods traffic from Monday 13th July 1964 and to passengers from Monday 7th November 1966. It was located 5½ miles from Ipswich, 3¾ miles from Manningtree, 11½ miles from Colchester and 63¼ miles from London Liverpool Street. The passenger service to Hadleigh was withdrawn by the London & North Eastern Railway (LNER) after the last train ran on Saturday 27th February 1932. Following the withdrawal of this service, Bentley became an intermediate station on this busy main line. The junction for the 7½ mile long railway line to Hadleigh was approximately ¾ mile north of Bentley and remained open for goods traffic for another 33 years, until closed by BR in April 1965. The Ipswich facing part of the junction was planned and indeed the cutting was dug but it is doubtful whether any regular passenger trains ran to Ipswich from Hadleigh. The Great Eastern Railway (GER) owned Dodnash Priory Farm at Bentley and this was visited by the Chairman of the company, Lord Claud Hamilton and other officials at Easter, Harvest, Christmas and during the shooting season. A siding, approximately ¾ miles south of Bentley and adjacent to Dobnash, existed until the 1920s. The farm was used as a rest home for the many horses employed by the GER on shunting and haulage duties at stations such as Woodbridge. Following the demolition of Bentley station, there is little evidence that it ever existed.

Blythburgh (Southwold Railway [narrow gauge])
This intermediate station was located 4 miles from Southwold and 5 miles from Halesworth on the 3ft. gauge Southwold - Halesworth railway line. It was advertised as the station for Wangford, which was stated as being 2¾ miles north of Blythburgh station. A bridge, demolished in 1960, carried the A12 trunk road over the railway at this point. Blythburgh opened in December 1879, and after the opening of the railway on Wednesday 24th September 1879. It closed completely from Friday 12th April 1929 with the closing of the line. The first winter timetable (December 1879) issued by the railway stated that trains stopped at Blythburgh by hand signal and passengers wishing to alight there must inform the Guard at the starting station. In 1908, an existing siding was converted to a passing loop allowing trains to pass there.

Bramford
An intermediate station, Bramford was on the railway line carrying services between Ipswich and Bury St. Edmunds, and from late 1849, services between Ipswich and Norwich Victoria (later diverted to Norwich Thorpe). Bramford is a village on the outskirts of Ipswich and the station was located 2½ miles from Ipswich, 43¾ miles from Norwich, 24 miles from Bury St. Edmunds and 71¼ miles from London Liverpool Street. Although not complete, Bramford was opened by the Ipswich, Bury and Norwich Railway (IB&NR) to goods on Monday 30th November 1846 and to passengers on Thursday 24th December 1846. In 1912, the wooden station was burnt out and rebuilt in brick. Bramford was closed completely by BR from Monday 2nd May 1955, a private siding remaining in use at that time.

Brampton / Brampton (Suffolk)
The line through Brampton was opened by the ESR to passengers on Monday 4th December 1854 and to goods traffic early in 1855. It was operated by the ECR, having been built by the Halesworth, Beccles & Haddiscoe Railway. This intermediate station remains open for passengers, but was closed by BR to goods traffic from Monday 13th July 1964. Brampton is on the Ipswich - Lowestoft railway line, and is located 4¾ miles from Beccles, 35¾ miles from Ipswich, 13¼ miles from Lowestoft and 104½ miles from London Liverpool Street. Prior to the closure of the direct line between Beccles and Yarmouth South Town in 1959, Brampton was 17¼ miles from Yarmouth South Town. The station is set in somewhat remote but pleasant rolling countryside and is nearer to the village of Redisham than Brampton. All the station buildings have been demolished and Brampton now consists of a single platform which prior to singling of the line was the up platform, and a bus-stop type shelter. After the closure of the former Midland & Great Northern Joint line in 1959, a waiting shelter from Great Ormesby station was moved to Brampton where it remained on the down platform until 1985, when it was acquired for preservation by the Mangapps Railway Museum, Burnham on Crouch, Essex. In June 1928, the station name was amended to Brampton (Suffolk) by which it continues to be known today.

Brandon / Brandon (Norfolk) / Brandon
Brandon is an intermediate station with a flint built station building and staggered platforms on the Norfolk/Suffolk border. It is on the Ely - Norwich railway line being 16 miles from Ely and 37½ miles from Norwich. The town of Brandon and part of the station is in Suffolk with the remainder in Norfolk. Brandon was opened on Wednesday 30th July 1845 by the ECR and the Norfolk Railway, the latter having been formed by the amalgamation of the Yarmouth and Norwich and the Norwich and Brandon Railways. With the line through Brandon being the original London to Norwich main line, the Norfolk Railway built a large engine shed at Brandon but by the end of 1848, this appears to have been taken out of use. In addition to the engine shed, Brandon was provided with large goods sheds, a goods yard on the down side of the track, sidings on the up side and an assortment of buildings including a bookstall on the up platform.

The station was renamed Brandon (Norfolk) on Sunday 1st July 1923 and reverted to Brandon on Sunday 1st March 1925. It became unstaffed from Tuesday 7th March 1967, and in recent years has seen a limited revival in goods traffic. The main station buildings still exist and have been used for number of purposes since they became surplus to railway needs. The "Friends of Brandon Station", a local volunteer group, hopes to restore the buildings some of which are of flint construction. One episode of the very popular "Dads Army" television comedy series includes scenes at Brandon station and in the goods yard.

Brockford & Wetheringsett (Mid Suffolk Light Railway)
This intermediate station was located 6 miles from Haughley and 13 miles from Laxfield on the light railway that ran between these two stations. The line opened to goods traffic on Tuesday 20th September 1904 but Brockford & Wetheringsett was not one of those stations providing a goods service at that time. Passenger services commenced at the station on Tuesday 29th September 1908. All services were withdrawn and the line closed by BR after the final passenger train ran on Saturday 26th July 1952. According to an eye witness who worked on the wartime airfield known as RAF Mendlesham / USAAF Station 156 in 1943, this station was the preferred choice by the airfield authorities for passenger and goods traffic, rather than that at Mendlesham.
The Mid Suffolk Light Railway Museum now exists on the site.

Bungay
Situated on the Tivetshall - Beccles railway line, Bungay was located 13 miles from Tivetshall, 6½ miles from Beccles and 27½ miles from Norwich via Tivetshall. This intermediate station had two platforms, quite extensive goods facilities and was one of the passing places on the single track Waveney Valley line. The station was opened by the Waveney Valley Railway (WVR) on Friday 2nd November 1860 following the completion of the railway between Harleston and Bungay. This was the second section of the WVR from Tivetshall to Beccles to be opened, the first being the Tivetshall to Harleston section in December 1855. The complete railway from Tivetshall to Beccles opened on Monday 2nd March 1863, when the WVR was amalgamated with the GER. A new water tower was built in 1931 and the wooden station buildings were replaced by a more substantial brick building which was completed in 1933. Bungay was closed to passengers by BR after the last train ran on Saturday 3rd January 1953 and goods traffic ceased from Monday 3rd August 1964. Although no trace remains of the station and railway at Bungay, one important part of the infrastructure lives on. The 5000 gallon water tank used to service steam locomotives at Bungay was dismantled in August 1972 and moved to the North Norfolk Railway (NNR). Amongst the locomotives nowadays using it is Class J15 0-6-0 No. 65462, once a frequent visitor to Bungay and now preserved in working order on the NNR. Weighing around 5 tons empty, the tank measures 16ft. x 8 ft. x 4ft. deep.

Bures
This intermediate station is on the Marks Tey - Sudbury railway line and at one time had a passing loop. Located on the Suffolk/Essex border, the station is 6¾ miles from Marks Tey, 5 miles from Sudbury and 53½ miles from London Liverpool Street. In 1960, prior to the withdrawal of passenger services on lines in the area north of Sudbury, Bures was 39¾ miles from Cambridge and 25½ miles from Bury St. Edmunds. The now demolished main station building had a bell housing on the roof; the bell being rung to notify passengers of the arrival of a train. Since the demolition of this fine building, passengers have used the wooden hut on the platform for shelter. This hut is a long standing feature of Bures and survived the demolition of the station buildings. The station serves the community of Bures which is made up of the parishes of Bures St. Mary and Bures Hamlet. The larger of the two, Bures St. Mary, is in Suffolk and Bures Hamlet is in Essex, as is the station.
Built by the Colchester, Stour Valley, Sudbury & Halstead Railway and opening on Monday 2nd July 1849, the line was leased to the Ipswich, Bury and Norwich Railway which later amalgamated with the EUR. Prior to the service being withdrawn from Monday 28th December 1964, goods traffic handled at Bures included timber, coal, farm produce, livestock and grain.

Bury St. Edmunds Northgate / Bury St. Edmunds
This large and impressive red brick building complete with stone dressings, has twin towers at the eastern end and initially had a train shed overall roof. It was built in the Elizabethan style as a terminus and originally had elegant tall brick chimneys, four tracks but only a single platform. The station was brought into use in November 1847 whilst still not quite complete, a temporary station having been provided for the opening of the IB&NR line from Haughley in December 1846. Shortly after the opening, the IB&NR amalgamated with the EUR. In April 1854, with the opening of the Newmarket line, Bury St. Edmunds became an intermediate station and in 1893,

the train shed overall roof was removed and replaced by canopies, and the chimneys reduced in height. For many years Bury St. Edmunds Northgate (now Bury St. Edmunds) had a fine refreshment room, run for part of the time by the Hotels Executive, serving a full range of breakfasts, luncheons, teas and dinners. Two railway lines from Bury St. Edmunds have closed, to the north a line ran to Thetford (for connections to Norwich) and to the south the other ran to Long Melford (for connections to London and Colchester via Marks Tey). The passenger service to Thetford was withdrawn in June 1953 and that to Long Melford in April 1961. In both cases, these lines were not immediately closed but remained open to goods traffic for some years. Bury St. Edmunds is served by services on the busy east/west cross country route from Ipswich to Peterborough, Ely and Cambridge with some through services to London Liverpool Street (95¼ miles), although at the time of writing the future of these services is uncertain. A wide area now separates the two remaining tracks through the station, the two central through lines having been recovered when the track layout was rationalised. Bury St. Edmunds is located 26½ miles from Ipswich, 29 miles from Cambridge via Newmarket and 28 miles from Ely. Prior to the withdrawal of the passenger services mentioned above, the station was 12¾ miles from Thetford, 16½ miles from Long Melford and just 78 miles from London Liverpool Street via Long Melford and Marks Tey. The motive power depot (31E) at Bury St. Edmunds officially closed in January 1959, by which time it was considered a sub shed of Cambridge depot (31A). Bury St. Edmunds station is a listed building and in recent years has been extensively refurbished.

Bury St. Edmunds Eastgate / Eastgate Street

Bury St. Edmunds Eastgate was an intermediate station on the Bury St. Edmunds Northgate - Long Melford railway line. It was opened by the GER on Wednesday 9th August 1865, closed to passengers by the GER from Sunday 1st May 1909 and to goods traffic by BR in 1960. Nothing remains of this station which was nearer to the town centre, Cathedral and Abbey Gardens than Northgate station.

Capel

Capel was an intermediate station situated close to the A12 trunk road on the Bentley - Hadleigh railway line. It served the parishes of Capel St Mary and Little Wenham. The station was located 2¼ miles from Bentley, 5 miles from Hadleigh and 65½ miles from London Liverpool Street. Although not complete, it was opened by the Eastern Union & Hadleigh Junction Railway for goods on Tuesday 21st August 1847, and for passengers on Thursday 2nd September 1847. The passenger service, which consisted in the 1920s of a weekday service of five trains each way and an extra down train on Saturdays, was withdrawn by the London and North Eastern Railway (LNER) after the last train on Saturday 27th February 1932. Goods continued to be handled at Capel until Monday 13th July 1964 when this service was withdrawn by BR, the public delivery siding having closed from Monday 2nd June 1958.

Cavendish

Cavendish was located on the Cambridge - Haverhill - Long Melford railway line 3¾ miles from Long Melford, 9¾ miles from Haverhill, 28 miles from Cambridge and 23½ miles from Colchester via Marks Tey. This intermediate station was opened by the GER on Wednesday 9th August 1865, closed to goods traffic from Monday 28th December 1964 and became unstaffed from Sunday 14th August 1966. One of the personalities at Cavendish was Bill Tharby, the local signalman who had worked on the railway for 53 years. The village has been described as the perfect picture postcard English village and has many nearby tourist attractions. In spite of these assets, the passenger service was withdrawn by BR from Monday 6th March 1967. In 2009, a small part of one of the platforms exists and the crossing keeper's house has been converted to a private residence and extended.

Clare

Clare was located on the Cambridge - Haverhill - Long Melford railway line 6½ miles from Long Melford, 7 miles from Haverhill, 25¼ miles from Cambridge and 26¼ miles from Colchester via Marks Tey. This intermediate station was opened by the GER on Wednesday 9th August 1865, closed to goods traffic by BR from Monday 12th September 1966, and to passengers from Monday 6th March 1967. A fine historic wool town, Clare is set in Constable Country and has many attractions including Clare Country Park where the well maintained former railway station (now used by the Park Rangers), the platforms and the good shed complete with a railway box van can be seen. The crane outside the goods shed was previously at Glemsford. A steam locomotive last visited Clare on the weekend of 15th-16th May 2004 when Class J15 0-6-0 No. 65462 from the North Norfolk Railway was on display in light steam in the former station yard.

Claydon
The official opening of the line by the Ipswich, Bury and Norwich Railway (IB&NR) through the uncompleted station at Claydon was Monday 7th December 1846, however the station opened to goods on Monday 30th November 1846 and to passengers on Thursday 24th December 1846, shortly before the IB&NR and the EUR amalgamated. The line initially carried services between Ipswich and Bury St. Edmunds, but from late 1849, has also handled services between Ipswich and Norwich (initially Norwich Victoria but later to Norwich Thorpe). Claydon was located 4¾ miles from Ipswich, 41½ miles from Norwich, 21¾ miles from Bury St. Edmunds and 73½ miles from London Liverpool Street. The station was closed to passengers by BR from Monday 17th June 1963 and to goods traffic from Saturday 31st March 1971 when the coal depot closed. A rail connected cement works existed near by. At the time of writing (2009), plans have been approved to build a new railway station, able to cater for intercity trains, at nearby Great Blakenham. The station is part of the "SnOasis" project which concerns the setting up of a ski centre, holiday resort and centre of winter sports excellence. Permission was granted for the station by the Secretary of State on Wednesday 7th May 2008.

Cockfield / Cockfield (Suffolk)
Cockfield was an intermediate station on the Bury St. Edmunds - Long Melford railway line and became Cockfield (Suffolk) on 1st October 1927. Opened by the GER on Wednesday 9th August 1865 the station was located 8 miles from Bury St. Edmunds, 8½ miles from Long Melford and 23¼ miles from Marks Tey. Cockfield was closed to passengers by BR from Monday 10th April 1961 and to goods traffic from Monday 19th April 1965. Despite being closed to passengers, the station did appear in the British Railways Timetable for the period 12th June to 10th September 1961 with passengers being advised that the locality was served by omnibuses. In 2009, Cockfield station building and platform exist but in a derelict state.

Corton
This intermediate station was on the Lowestoft Central - Yarmouth railway line, one of two lines in East Anglia built by the Norfolk & Suffolk Joint Railways Committee, a joint venture by the GER and the Midland & Great Northern Joint Railway (M&GN). It was located 3½ miles from Lowestoft Central, 6¾ miles from Yarmouth South Town, 8¾ miles from Yarmouth Beach (all services withdrawn in 1953) and 121¼ miles from London Liverpool Street via Lowestoft Central and Beccles. With through expresses from the Midlands and London, in the heyday of the holiday camps Corton could be very busy on summer Saturdays with hundreds of holiday makers arriving and departing. In addition, passenger traffic was further boosted by the Camping Coaches that could be found in the loading dock. Now used as a private residence, it is the only station building between Lowestoft and Yarmouth to survive in the 21st century, all others being demolished to make way for new development. However, the majority of the former railway land around the station has now been built on. Corton opened on Monday 13th July 1903 and was closed by BR to goods traffic from Monday 13th July 1964 and to passengers after the last train from Yarmouth South Town ran on Saturday 2nd May 1970. The station had been unstaffed since Monday 12th September 1966. Bridge No. 2428 still exists to the south of the station as does the former station master's house.

Cratfield (Mid Suffolk Light Railway - Goods Only)
Cratfield was intended to be an intermediate station between Laxfield and Huntingfield on the MSLR cross country line to Halesworth. However, the railway never ventured past Cratfield which became a goods only destination. The line east of Laxfield station from Laxfield Mill to Cratfield closed in 1912 and was lifted two years later.

Darsham
Opened by the ESR on Wednesday 1st June 1859 and operated by the ECR from that date, this intermediate station is situated on the Ipswich - Lowestoft railway line and adjacent to the A12 trunk road. Darsham became unstaffed from Monday 6th March 1967 and closed to goods traffic from Monday 19th April 1965. It is located 13¾ miles from Beccles, 26¾ miles from Ipswich, 22¼ miles from Lowestoft and 95½ miles from London Liverpool Street. Whilst not in railway use, the station buildings on the down platform remain as does the shelter on the up platform. Darsham was noted in timetables for many years as the station for the nearby village of Yoxford. It was also favoured by many travellers as the station for Southwold, the journey between Darsham and Southwold being in a horse drawn or motor omnibus and preferred to using the Southwold Railway via Halesworth.

Debenham (Mid Suffolk Light Railway - Goods Only)
Debenham was intended to be an intermediate station between

Kenton and Framsden on the MSLR line from Kenton to Westerfield. In similar circumstances to Cratfield, the railway never ventured past Debenham which only ever handled goods traffic.

Sections of embankment and remains of the railway bridge over the B1077 road north of Debenham in late 2009.

The line to Debenham closed in 1906 and was lifted in 1914, in spite of this; remains of the line are easy to locate today.

Derby Road / Derby Road (Ipswich)

Derby Road is an intermediate station serving the eastern side of Ipswich, and was one of the original stations opened on Tuesday 1st May 1877 by the Felixstowe Railway and Pier Company (FR&PC) on the new railway between Westerfield and Felixstowe Pier. The station was originally served by Westerfield - Felixstowe Beach - Felixstowe Pier services, but with numerous changes to the branch line over the years it is now served by Ipswich - Westerfield - Felixstowe (previously Felixstowe Town) passenger services. Regular freight traffic passes through Derby Road which is located 2½ miles from Westerfield, 9¾ miles from Felixstowe (Town) and 74¾ miles from London Liverpool Street. In addition to sidings once used for coal and scrap metal traffic, about 1 mile beyond the station there once existed private sidings serving the industrial premises of Crane Ltd. and Ransomes, Sims and Jefferies Ltd. In the years leading up to it becoming unstaffed, Station Master R.A. Rowland was in charge at Derby Road and in the booking office, where in 1961 a total of 46,994 tickets were sold, we could usually find Chief Clerk Mr. P. Meakings. The station often won the first class prize in the station gardens competition, much of the work to achieve this being carried out by Signalman F. Hines, who was at one time Porter/Shunter at the station. In distance terms, as the crow flies the station at Derby Road is approximately 2 miles from Ipswich station but by rail, it is 6miles. The Ipswich tramway ventured to Derby Road station and provided a more direct route to the town centre than the railway.

Elmswell

The intermediate station at Elmswell is on the busy east/west cross country railway line carrying services between Peterborough, Ely, Cambridge, Newmarket, Bury St. Edmunds and Ipswich. In addition to private sidings to the timber yard, sawmill and bacon factory, an unusual aspect of Elmswell was the tramline to Woolpit brickworks. During World War II, materials, including bombs, were handled at Elmswell for Great Ashfield airfield. The official opening of the line by the Ipswich, Bury and Norwich Railway (IB&NR) through the uncompleted station was on Monday 7th December 1846. Elmswell opened to goods on Monday 30th November 1846 and to passengers on Thursday 24th December 1846, shortly before the IB&NR and the EUR amalgamated. The station closed to goods traffic from Monday 28th December 1964. It is located 37¾ miles from Cambridge, 17¾ miles from Ipswich and 86½ miles from London Liverpool Street. The station became unstaffed from Monday 2nd January 1967 and the main building on the down platform was demolished in the early 1970s and replaced by a bus-stop type shelter. On the up platform the canopied waiting room has been retained in non railway use and the canopy provides some shelter for rail users. During the war with Egypt and consequent petrol rationing in 1957, the Suffolk Hunt chartered a train to return the hounds, horses, huntsmen and followers from Elmswell to Bury St. Edmunds. The Hunt had been taken from Bury St. Edmunds to Mellis earlier in the day by special train.

Eye

The eastern terminus of the 3 mile long railway line from Mellis, Eye was opened on Tuesday 2nd April 1867 by the Mellis & Eye Railway Company. In 1898, the GER officially absorbed the Mellis & Eye Railway Company having operated the line for many years. The distance from Eye to Norwich was 26½ miles and to London Liverpool Street it was 94½ miles. In the 1920s, the passenger service consisted of five trains each way on Mondays and four trains each way on other weekdays. This service was withdrawn by the LNER from Monday 2nd February 1931, but it was not until Monday 13th July 1964 that BR closed the line to goods traffic. There was a small brick built engine shed at Eye which had basic locomotive servicing facilities and this closed after the withdrawal of the passenger service.

Felixstowe / Felixstowe Beach
Although not quite complete, this intermediate station was one of the original stations opened on Tuesday 1st May 1877 by the Felixstowe Railway and Pier Company (FR&PC) on the new railway between Westerfield and Felixstowe Pier. Felixstowe Beach was considered the main station for Felixstowe and records show that it was known as Felixstowe and also Felixstowe Town until the new Town station opened in July 1898, whereupon it became known as Beach station. An engine shed, which was a sub shed of Ipswich (32B), and a large carriage paint shop once existed at Felixstowe Beach. By 1950, locomotive servicing had been transferred to Town station and no real evidence existed of the paint shop which apparently had been destroyed by fire many years earlier. In the final years before closure, the station was only open in the summer months. Beach station became unstaffed from Monday 12th September 1966, was closed to goods traffic from Monday 5th December 1966, and closed to passengers from Monday 11th September 1967. Despite many protests, the disused station building was demolished in April 2004. Today, some of the trains serving the Port of Felixstowe pass through the station site.

Felixstowe Pier
Opened by the FR&PC on Tuesday 1st May 1877, Felixstowe Pier was the last passenger station on the original railway line from Westerfield to Felixstowe. It was closed by the LNER from Monday 11th September 1939, reopened by them on Monday 3rd June 1946 and closed permanently by BR from Monday 2nd July 1951. In addition to the closeness to the railway pier and dock, an important aspect of Pier station from 1912 was the easy access to the boarding point for the GER, London & North Eastern Railway and BR operated boats such as the *Pin Mill, Hainault, Epping* and *Brightlingsea* that provided the ferry service to Shotley and Harwich. This allowed passengers to travel by rail and boat with ease to these destinations, a trip often undertaken by this author. Pier station was one of the stations in Suffolk where Camping Coaches were located for use as accommodation for holiday makers. Some private goods sidings existed in the vicinity of Pier station and the dock, and today the line previously serving this station forms one of the rail access points into the vast Felixstowe Dock and Railway Company estate. The port generates a vast of volume of freight, and in 2007 an £85m plan was announced by Hutchinson, the port operator, to expand the port and increase the amount of freight carried by rail. Felixstowe is considered the largest UK container port and in addition to access through this former station site, it has another rail access point near Trimley.

Felixstowe Town / Felixstowe
Opened by the Great Eastern Railway (GER) on Friday 1st July 1898, Felixstowe Town was a large well laid out station more centrally located than the other two stations in the town. An addition to the original FR&PC Westerfield - Felixstowe Pier railway, the opening ceremony was attended by Lord Claud Hamilton and fellow directors of the GER. Track was laid in 1898 and the original 1877 railway line diverted to access the new town centre site. Following this change to the track layout, trains requiring access to the stations at Felixstowe Beach and Pier, and the dock area, had to reverse at the new station. In later years this included trains conveying large quantities of containers both from Ipswich and the docks – all had to reverse to continue their journey. In April 1970, with the need to improve the railway to the port area, changes in the track layout saw this access abolished and the 1877 direct line to the docks from Westerfield and Ipswich reinstated. The short section of track from the 1877 line to Town station originally laid in 1898 was retained and other track laid in 1898 was recovered and the land sold. Felixstowe Town is the passenger terminus of the 12¼ mile railway line from Westerfield and has been unstaffed from Saturday 12th September 1966. Since Thursday 20th February 1969 the terminus has been known as Felixstowe. Now used for passenger services only to Ipswich, the present single platform is only part of one of the longer original platforms and is separated from the former station complex by a car park entrance road which rail passengers have to cross the reach the platform. Since 1984 many of the former station buildings and rooms have been in use as restaurants or shops and the adjacent railway land is used for roads, car parking or a weekly market. The GER acquired the Felix Hotel, considered the best hotel on the east coast, on 21st June 1920. This

remained in railway ownership until the spring of 1952, when it was disposed of by the Hotels Executive.

Delivering the goods at Felixstowe in the 1950s. Transferring this petrol tank from rail to road transport are Leading Porter Brown on the left and Road Motor Driver Richmond on the right.

At one time Felixstowe Town had a large goods yard and shed, locomotive turntable and Camping Coaches sited in sidings close by the station toilets. Goods traffic ceased at this station from Monday 5th December 1966 but traffic to and from the docks continued to use it for reversal purposes until the original 1877 line to Beach and Pier stations and the docks was reinstated. Felixstowe is 15¾ miles from Ipswich and 84½ miles from London Liverpool Street, and at one time through trains to and from the capital were a regular occurrence. In the early 1960s, Station Master S. Rowbury was in charge of both remaining Felixstowe stations and Trimley. Amongst the staff at Town station at that time were Station Foreman B.A. Saberton, Porters G. E. Jennings and L. Proudley, Leading Porter C.J. Patey, Motor Driver M. Beamish and Leading Porter Brown, who worked in the summer at Beach station. The "Felixstowe Town" nameboard from the signal box can be seen at Bressingham Steam Museum.

Finningham

This intermediate station was located 17¾ miles from Ipswich and 28½ miles from Norwich Thorpe on the Ipswich - Norwich Thorpe railway line. The station, albeit a temporary structure and later replaced by a permanent building, was opened by the EUR to goods on Wednesday 7th June 1848. Finningham was closed by BR to goods traffic from Sunday 28th November 1964 and to passengers from Monday 7th November 1966. The line to Norwich opened in late 1849 and initially, the terminus there for passenger trains stopping at or passing through Finningham was Victoria station, however within a few years they were moved to Thorpe station.

Framlingham

Well known for the fine castle, mere and delightful old buildings, Framlingham was the terminus of a 6½ mile single track railway from Wickham Market. Opened with the ESR on Wednesday 1st June 1859 and operated by the ECR from that date, the station was closed to passengers by BR after the last train ran on Saturday 1st November 1952. For a number of years following the closure of the line to "ordinary" passengers, special trains were run between Framlingham and London at the start and end of term for pupils attending Framlingham College. The last recorded passenger train to Framlingham was a rambler's excursion from London Liverpool Street on Good Friday 12th April 1963 hauled by Class 31 AIA-AIA No. D5595. Goods traffic continued to be handled for many years and was finally withdrawn from Easter Monday 19th April 1965, the last scheduled train being hauled by Class 24 Bo-Bo No. D5047 on Thursday 15th April. Framlingham served a large catchment area of rural Suffolk and the often lightly loaded passenger trains were compensated for by a considerable amount of goods traffic generated by the agricultural community. The station was 91 miles from London Liverpool Street and 22¼ miles from Ipswich. A daily service of four passenger trains each way with no services on Sundays is shown in the 1952 timetable for Framlingham. There was a small engine shed at Framlingham complete with a coaling stage and watering facilities which was a sub shed of Ipswich (32B). The former station building still exists and externally appears little altered from the days when it was the town station.

Glemsford

Glemsford was an intermediate station located on the Cambridge - Haverhill - Long Melford railway line 2½ miles from Long Melford, 11 miles from Haverhill, 29¼ miles from Cambridge and 22¼ miles from Colchester via Marks Tey.

The station was opened by the GER on Wednesday 9th August 1865 and became unstaffed from Monday 15th August 1966. Goods passing through Glemsford included many unusual products derived from the local horsehair processing industry. Glemsford closed to goods traffic from Monday 12th September 1966 and passenger services were withdrawn by BR from Monday 6th March 1967. Both the former station house and goods shed still exist, and have been converted for residential use. In 2009, one level crossing gate still existed in a broken condition. The goods crane from Glemsford can now be found outside Clare goods shed, which is in Clare Castle Country Park.

Hacheston Halt

This intermediate halt was between Marlesford and Parham Halt on the Wickham Market - Framlingham railway line and opened in the 1920s. Closed by BR from Monday 3rd November 1952 the halt was located 3¼ miles from Wickham Market and 3¼ miles from Framlingham. It was a very basic stopping place for trains with passengers wishing to join or alight from the train, being provided with steps. The facilities consisted of one oil lamp, the station nameboard, and planks or recovered sleepers to walk on.

Hadleigh

Hadleigh station was opened by the Eastern Union & Hadleigh Junction Railway for goods on Saturday 21st August 1847 and passengers on Thursday 2nd September 1847 as the terminus of the 7¼ mile long railway from Bentley. A small attractive market town close to the Essex/Suffolk border, the railway station at Hadleigh was 11 miles from Manningtree, 18¾ miles from Colchester and 70½ miles from London Liverpool Street. The passenger service, which consisted in the 1920s of five trains each way weekdays and an extra down train on Saturdays, was withdrawn by the London & North Eastern Railway (LNER) after the last train ran on Saturday 27th February 1932. Hadleigh continued to handle goods traffic until Monday 19th April 1965 when the line was closed by BR, one of the last trains being hauled by Class 31 AIA-AIA No. D5634. The station yard was dominated by large maltings and the outward goods traffic was predominantly agricultural. Hadleigh had locomotive servicing facilities and a small wooden engine shed until the withdrawal of the passenger service, after which the shed appears to have been closed and the structure dismantled.

Halesworth

Halesworth is a small busy market town with an intermediate station on the Ipswich - Lowestoft railway line. The present station was not the first to serve the locality, this was located about ¼ mile further north and built as part of the Halesworth, Beccles and Haddiscoe Railway, which became the ESR and operated by the ECR. The first station opened to goods traffic during November 1854 and to passengers on Monday 4th December 1854 as the southern terminus of the line from Haddiscoe, and is remembered today in Halesworth with the presence of Old Station Road which is off Norwich Road. The present station dates from 1859 when the line from Halesworth was extended south to Ipswich via Woodbridge. Halesworth is 100¾ miles from London Liverpool Street, 32 miles from Ipswich, 17 miles from Lowestoft and until the withdrawal of services, was 21 miles from Yarmouth South Town (via St. Olaves) and 9 miles from Southwold. In 1901, the intention was to build a railway (the Mid Suffolk Light Railway) from Haughley to Halesworth. However, the track never did get any further east from Haughley than Cratfield.

Now demolished and replaced by a road and residential development, a large railway served dairy was once situated behind the up platform and generated much rail borne milk traffic until it closed in 1965. This was in addition to the general goods handled at this station that justified many sidings, a large goods shed and a regular visit from a locomotive to shunt there. Goods traffic was handled at Halesworth until Monday 19th April 1965 and the station became unstaffed from Monday 6th March 1967. From 1879 until 1929, Halesworth provided interchange and transhipping facilities between the national railway network and the narrow gauge Southwold Railway. Passengers arriving or boarding at the Southwold Railway station and needing to gain access to the GER/LNER could cross from the Southwold Railway station platform by a footbridge to the south end of the GER/LNER station platforms. During World War II, Halesworth handled substantial traffic for the wartime airfields in the local area. An unusual feature of the present station is the moveable part of the platforms. No longer in use, these were installed in 1887, renewed in 1922 and refurbished in 1999. The movable sections were necessary due to the need to provide longer platforms for the increasingly longer trains, and in the case of Halesworth, this involved crossing a main road. These sections allowed the platforms to be extended across the road thereby forming a long continuous platform. When not required for rail passengers, the moveable platform sections were swung to one side to open the road for traffic, and formed a level crossing. The moveable platform sections became redundant when a road bridge was constructed nearby over the railway in 1959 and the main Norwich Road diverted. Today they remain permanently fixed and form part of the station platforms that are not in general use. The redundant signal box was moved to a nearby school playing field where it resided for several years and in 2007 was moved to the Mid Norfolk Railway's County School station.

Halesworth (Southwold Railway [narrow gauge])
Located behind the Halesworth GER/LNER up platform this station was the western terminus of the 9 mile long narrow gauge Southwold Railway. Complete with a transhipment platform, Halesworth (SR) station opened on Wednesday 24th September 1879, and closed to passengers after the final train ran on Thursday 11th April 1929. A small engine shed was built in 1914 at Halesworth, a short distance from the station and like the station, no trace now remains of this building. The most noticeable remnant of the Southwold Railway at Halesworth is one of the bridge abutments which was part of the girder bridge carrying the railway over Holton Road. The girders were removed in March 1962 and the abutment on the station side of the road has been removed. This bridge was adjacent to the existing railway bridge carrying the Ipswich - Lowestoft railway over the same road.

Haughley Road (Ipswich, Bury and Norwich Railway)
This intermediate station was between Stowmarket and Elmswell on the Ipswich - Bury St. Edmunds line which was officially opened by the Ipswich, Bury and Norwich Railway (IB&NR) on Monday 7th December 1846, however, the station opened to goods on Monday 30th November 1846 and to passengers on Thursday 24th December 1846, shortly before the IB&NR and the EUR amalgamated. Haughley Road closed from Monday 9th July 1849 having been replaced by the new Haughley Junction station.

Haughley Junction / Haughley Road (Great Eastern Railway) / **Haughley / Haughley West / Haughley**
This junction station opened on Monday 2nd July 1849 and was brought into use on Monday 9th July by the EUR as Haughley Junction with lines running north to Norwich, west to Bury St. Edmunds, Cambridge, and Ely, and south to Ipswich. The line to Bury St. Edmunds, Ely, and Cambridge left the Norwich line north of this station. In 1866, whilst under GER control, the station was renamed Haughley Road and in 1890 was again renamed this time as Haughley. Under LNER control in July 1923, the name was changed to Haughley West and finally in September 1932 it reverted to Haughley, the name under which it was closed by BR to goods traffic on 28th December 1964 and to passengers from 2nd January 1967. From September 1932 until Saturday 26th July 1952, the former MSLR line to Laxfield terminated at this station, having moved from the adjacent MSLR station. During the existence of the MSLR, the line left the north end of the station site and headed east. Haughley was 83 miles from London Liverpool Street, 32 miles from Norwich Thorpe, 14¼ miles from Ipswich and 12¼ miles from Bury St. Edmunds. The Haughley Silo was a giant structure close to the station. This prominent landmark was completed and officially brought into use during August 1951, and was demolished during October 2008.

Haughley / Haughley East (Mid Suffolk Light Railway)
Located adjacent to the main line station, this was the western terminus of the 19 mile single track Mid Suffolk Light Railway (MSLR) line from Laxfield. The MSLR station opened to goods traffic in September 1904 and to passengers four years later.
In 1923, the MSLR passed to the LNER and in 1932, the passenger and goods services were combined with the main line station. The station was known as Haughley East for a brief period following the transfer of the MSLR to the LNER. BR closed the former MSLR after the last train ran on Saturday 26th July 1952.

Haverhill / Haverhill North
This Great Eastern Railway (GER) station was on the Cambridge - Long Melford railway line and opened to Cambridge on Thursday 1st June 1865. It was located 18¼ miles from Cambridge, and from Tuesday 8th August 1865, 13½ miles from Long Melford, 28¼ miles from Marks Tey and 33¼ miles from Colchester. Originally Haverhill, the station became Haverhill North from Sunday 1st July 1923, but reverted to Haverhill in May 1952. A connection between Haverhill North and the Colne Valley and Halstead Railway (CV&HR) was opened by the GER in August 1865, the station thereby becoming a junction for the CV&HR. The CV&HR was a railway originating at Chappel and served several villages in Essex before terminating at Haverhill (CV&HR) station. It remained independent until 1923 when it was absorbed by the LNER. Haverhill became unstaffed from Sunday 14th August 1966 and

was closed by BR to goods traffic from Monday 31st October 1966. Passenger services were withdrawn and the line closed from Monday 6th March 1967. In the 1950s, Haverhill was designated a London overspill town and in spite of the planned large population increase, all railway services were withdrawn. Nothing remains of the station and the site is now owned by Tesco.

Haverhill / Haverhill South (Colne Valley & Halstead Railway)
Opening on Sunday 10th May 1863, this was the Haverhill terminus of the 19½ mile long CV&HR. A connection between the CV&HR and the GER Haverhill station was opened by the GER in August 1865. The distance from Haverhill to Chappel station in Essex by the CV&HR was 19½ miles compared to the longer GER route via Long Melford which was 24¾miles. Haverhill (CV&HR), by then known as Haverhill South, closed to passengers from Sunday 14th July 1924, CV&HR passenger services having been diverted to the LNER Haverhill (North) station. The station became a goods depot and remained in use until closed by BR from Monday 19th April 1965. Nothing remains of Haverhill South, the site now being under a private car park.

Higham

Higham was an intermediate station on the Bury St. Edmunds - Newmarket railway line. Opening on Saturday 1st April 1854, it was built by the Newmarket & Chesterford Railway and operated from the outset by the ECR. Higham was located 6½ miles from Bury St. Edmunds, 33 miles from Ipswich, 22½ miles from Cambridge and 21½ miles from Ely. BR withdrew goods facilities at Higham from Monday 28th December 1964 and passenger services were withdrawn from Monday 2nd January 1967. The main building was on the north or down side of the line, which was originally single track and later doubled.

Horham (Mid Suffolk Light Railway)
This intermediate station was located 14 miles from Haughley and 5 miles from Laxfield on the light railway that ran between these two stations. Horham opened to goods traffic on Tuesday 20th September 1904 and passenger services commenced at the station on Tuesday 29th September 1908. The final passenger train ran on the line on Saturday 26th July 1952 after which the line was closed by BR. The timber frame and corrugated iron clad station building was on the up side of the main MSLR line. This was acquired in 1987 from the original site by the Mangapps Farm Railway Museum, and it is now in use as Mangapps station at the museum.

Ingham

The intermediate station serving this small village was located 3¾ miles from Bury St. Edmunds and 9 miles from Thetford on the Bury St. Edmunds Northgate - Thetford railway line. Ingham was opened on Wednesday 1st March 1876 by the Bury St. Edmunds & Thetford Railway and closed to passengers by BR from Monday 8th June 1953. Goods traffic was handled there until Monday 27th June 1960. Like some other small rural Suffolk stations, Ingham was never a busy station except during both World Wars. The station building is now a private house. The weekday only service for the last summer that the line was open to passengers (1952) consisted of four trains each way with an additional train on Saturday evenings.

Ipswich

Ipswich is one of East Anglia's more important railway centres with lines running south west to serve Colchester, Chelmsford and London, north east to serve Lowestoft, Felixstowe and, until 1959, Yarmouth, and north west to serve Norwich, Bury St. Edmunds, Ely, Cambridge and the Midlands. The main part of the present station, which opened in 1860, was constructed jointly by the Eastern Union Railway (EUR) and the IB&NR, the plans being approved by a joint committee of directors from the two companies. The island platform, on the down side of the main line, was a later addition being completed in 1883. An earlier station of a temporary nature was opened in June 1846 by the EUR at Croft Street, this was closed on 1st July 1860 with the opening of the new station. Ipswich is 26½ miles from Bury St. Edmunds, 49 miles from Lowestoft, 68¾ miles from London Liverpool Street, 17 miles from Colchester, 46¼ miles from Norwich, 54½ miles from Ely and 55½ miles from Cambridge. An extensive dockside railway tramway existed at Ipswich serving a wide range of industries, but in recent years with the regeneration of the Wet Dock and New Cut areas for leisure, educational and residential use, almost the entire waterfront rail network has been recovered or covered over. On a survey undertaken in late 2009, only a few sections of isolated track could be found in public access areas. The Bridge Street level crossing appeared intact, but track either side of the crossing was covered over or cut through. The West Bank/Griffin Wharf rail terminal, accessed from Halifax Junction on the main line to London Liverpool Street, remains open predominantly for sand and aggregate but other goods/freight have been handled there in recent times such as steel.

Steam crane No. 279 assisting with track relaying at Ipswich in the 1950s.

A reminder of the past dock tramway can be found in New Cut West, where a short section of tramway style track can be found set in attractive red paving alongside the roadway. This is used in conjunction with trains using Griffin Wharf. The EUR, ECR and GER had important maritime interests in the docks through the steamers they chartered, owned or operated. Some of these vessels with names such as *Railway*, *Prince*, *Orion*, *Orwell*, *River Queen*, *Cardinal Wolsey*, *Atalanta*, *Ipswich*, *Suffolk*, *Norfolk* and *Essex*, became well known on the River Orwell. The Lower Goods Yard, referred to on some maps as "Goods Station", was officially closed by Network Rail on Monday 9th February 2009. The closure was the subject of a government document dated Tuesday 14th October 2008 and issued as part of the project associated with the expansion of freight services to Felixstowe port and rearrangement of the siding space at Ipswich. A large steam shed (32B) and later diesel locomotive depot existed at Croft Street, separated from the 1860 station by Stoke Hill tunnel. The last steam locomotives based there in the early 1960s were used as carriage steam heating units. In the 1930s, in addition to the locomotive depot, the congested Croft Street site was also home to a wagon works, offices, a high water tower, vast stacks of coal and a turntable. Many of the buildings were demolished in 1978 and following further recent clearance of the site, it is now occupied by housing. Some of the last uses for Croft Street were as the Ipswich Carriage and Wagon Shops and the CM & EE electrification depot. The complex nature and vastness of the docks railway system led to locomotives working a considerable distance from Ipswich shed, and a small locomotive shed complete with servicing facilities was established nearer the dock area. This shed became redundant when the Class J70 steam tram locomotives were replaced by 153hp Class DY1 diesel shunters.

Introduced at Ipswich in 1962, this two stage cleaning plant washed, scrubbed and rinsed locomotives that passed through each stage at 3mph.

These were later replaced by more powerful Class DJ12 diesel shunters. By 1955 at least four diesel shunters, Nos. 11500/1/2 and 11100 were allocated to Ipswich and were often to be found on the waterfront. Other steam locomotives did venture into dockland when the tram locomotives were unavailable and these were generally 0-6-0 tank locomotives, sometimes modified to 2-4-0 or 0-4-2 by the removal of coupling rods. Further steam locomotive servicing facilities existed adjacent to Ipswich station island platform and these included three engine sidings, pits with gas lighting, a turntable, water tanks and coaling stage. Used at one time for carriage sidings, they are today used for the stabling of electric freight locomotives, diesel multiple units and the stabling and refueling of diesel freight locomotives. Freight company Freightliner has offices adjacent to the sidings and another freight company, DB Schenker (EWS), has a signing on point there. Often an impressive array of locomotives, perhaps the largest in East Anglia, can be seen here awaiting their turn to haul heavy trains of rail borne containers and other goods to and from Felixstowe and destinations in the UK.

Kenton Junction / Kenton (Mid Suffolk Light Railway)
Kenton was an intermediate station with a passing loop on the light railway that ran between Haughley and Laxfield. Located 10 miles from Haughley and 9 miles from Laxfield, Kenton was the only station on the MSLR to have two passenger platforms. The station opened to goods traffic on Tuesday 20th September 1904 and to passengers four years later, on Tuesday 29th September 1908. It was planned in 1901 to construct a railway from Kenton to Westerfield on the Great Eastern Railway line between Ipswich and Beccles. However, despite a ceremony at Westerfield in 1902 to officially start the construction, the line was never built. Only a short section, from Kenton to Debenham ever existed and this was recovered during World War 1. The final passenger train left Kenton on Saturday 26th July 1952 after which the line was closed.

Lakenheath
Lakenheath is an intermediate station situated in an isolated location approximately 3 miles from the village of Lakenheath, 41½ miles from Norwich, 12 miles from Ely and 26¾ miles from Cambridge. The station is on the Norwich - Ely railway line and was opened by the ECR on Wednesday 30th July 1845. The goods shed has been demolished as have the buildings on the up platform where a small waiting shelter has been provided for passengers' use. In the mid 1860s, a short goods only line to a local quarry left the Norwich - Ely line in the vicinity of Lakenheath station in a northerly direction and another, a narrow gauge railway, once existed to Feltwell aerodrome but closed after World War 1. Lakenheath closed to goods traffic from Monday 12th September 1966 and became unstaffed from Tuesday 7th March 1967. The station sees minimal usage with the latest timetable showing no services Monday - Friday, one each way on Saturday and three each way on Sunday with all trains stopping by request only. Near to the station is the large RSPB Lakenheath Fen nature reserve and the weekend opening of the station provides easy access to this attraction for visitors. Lakenheath is near to a large military air base and adjacent to the B1112 road where a level crossing exists.

Lavenham
Situated on the Bury St. Edmunds Northgate - Long Melford railway line, Lavenham was located 11¼ miles from Bury St. Edmunds, 5¼ miles from Long Melford and just 66¾ miles from London Liverpool Street via Marks Tey. This intermediate station was opened by the GER on Wednesday 9th August 1865 and BR closed the station to passengers from Monday 10th April 1961. The track between Long Melford and Lavenham was taken up in 1962 making Lavenham a terminus with goods services to the town continuing to run from Bury St. Edmunds. These ceased from Monday 19th April 1965, the last train running on Thursday 15th April and hauled by Class 15 Bo-Bo No. D8221. A major tourist destination, Lavenham is described as one of the finest medieval towns in England with ancient streets, Tudor houses and crooked cottages. The town's railway station and goods facilities were kept busy with the sugar beet factory, flour mill, gas works, and coconut matting and horsehair fabric production all generating much traffic. Private sidings existed to the larger railway users with premises close to the railway. The "Hat" goods, a single van train, was one unusual aspect of the railway at Lavenham in the 1950s. This picked up for onward distribution, large flamboyant hats made locally. On Saturday 2nd June 1962, special passenger trains arrived at Lavenham from London Liverpool Street hauled by Class 31 AIA-AIA diesel locomotives. These conveyed over 800 guests for the wedding of Miss Anne Howard and Mr. Patrick Wolridge-Gordon, a Scottish MP, at the church. The trains were first class throughout with full catering facilities and the returning guests were the very last passengers to travel by train from Lavenham. After closure, the station house existed for many years but was eventually demolished to make way for an industrial building. Despite being closed to passengers, Lavenham did appear in the British Railways Timetable for the period 12th June - 10th September 1961 with passengers being advised that the locality was served by omnibuses. The bridge next to the station site carrying

the A1141 road over the track bed still exists and some of the track bed has been transformed into a pathway entitled "The Lavenham Walk".

Laxfield (Mid Suffolk Light Railway)
Laxfield formed the eastern passenger terminus of the single track MSLR line from Haughley. The station opened to goods traffic on Tuesday 20th September 1904 and to passengers four years later, on Tuesday 29th September 1908. Laxfield was located 19 miles from Haughley and 102 miles from London Liverpool Street. A small engine shed with servicing facilities once existed at Laxfield, this being a sub shed of Ipswich (32B) whilst under BR ownership. Originally it was proposed to extend the MSLR from Laxfield through to Halesworth on the Great Eastern Railway line between Ipswich and Beccles. Only a short section from Laxfield Mill, which was east of Laxfield station, to Cratfield ever existed and this was abandoned in 1912 and recovered during World War I. In the last month of operation, the weekday only passenger service consisted of one morning and one afternoon train from Laxfield to Haughley and the same from Haughley to Laxfield. By catching the 7.21am train from Laxfield, it was possible to arrive at Norwich Thorpe by 9.43am or at London Liverpool Street by 11.18am. For many years a through train ran between Stowmarket and Laxfield and vice versa for school children. The MSLR officially passed to the LNER in January 1923 and subsequently to BR, who closed the line after the last train ran on Saturday 26th July 1952. Following the closure, Laxfield station building was moved and became a sports pavilion on a playing field at a village near Framlingham. In 1991, it was purchased and restored by Mangapps Farm Railway Museum where it now serves as Old Heath Station.

Leiston
This intermediate station was located 2¼ miles from Thorpeness, 4¼ miles from Aldeburgh and 4 miles from Saxmundham on the Aldeburgh - Saxmundham railway line. Opened by the ESR on Wednesday 1st June 1859 and operated by the ECR from that date, the station was the original terminus of the line from Saxmundham, but within 12 months the line had been extended through to Aldeburgh. Many sidings and a railway tramway to the extensive Richard Garrett engineering works existed at Leiston, these works having internal rail access to many locations. The tramway was originally worked by horses, but these were replaced by the small steam shunting locomotive *Sirapite* in 1929, this in turn was replaced by a battery driven locomotive in 1962. The tramway was recovered by a Norwich scrap metal dealer in the late 1960s. A further tramway existed at Leiston which ran from the brickworks located north of the town and initially crossed the Aldeburgh line east of the station level crossing, and then joined the Garrett tramway. This was later altered to avoid crossing the Aldeburgh line. The brickworks closed in the mid 1920s. Track work remains in place through Leiston to approximately 1 mile east of the station site where facilities exist to serve the French owned British Energy nuclear power station at Sizewell. Leiston station building and the goods shed still survive and are privately owned. In addition to the infrequent trains serving the power station, a number of special passenger trains carrying mainly enthusiasts have traversed this remaining part of the line that at one time ventured to Aldeburgh, and was closed by BR to passengers after the last train ran on Saturday 10th September 1966. Goods traffic, mainly in the form of coal, was handled at Leiston until Monday 7th May 1984. Garrett's locomotive *Sirapite* can be seen at the Long Shop Museum in the town, this museum being housed in buildings that were once part of the Richard Garrett & Co. Ltd. Town Works. Garrett & Co. were once owned by Beyer, Peacock and Co. Ltd. of Gorton, Manchester and part of the Garrett estate, the Station Works, remained active until 1985 when final closure took place.

Melford / Long Melford
Long Melford was an important junction station with lines running west to Haverhill and Cambridge, north to Bury St. Edmunds and south to Sudbury and Marks Tey (for Colchester and London). Although not complete, the station was opened by the GER on Wednesday 9th August 1865, initially being known as Melford. It became Long Melford from Friday 1st February 1884. An indication of the importance in railway terms of this location was that a turntable was installed there. The Bury St. Edmunds - Long Melford line was closed by BR to passengers from Monday 10th April 1961 and to goods traffic (Bury St. Edmunds - Lavenham only) from Monday 19th April 1965. Following this closure, Long Melford became an intermediate station on the Cambridge - Haverhill - Sudbury - Marks Tey cross country route. Long Melford became unstaffed from Monday 15th August 1966 and closed to goods traffic from Monday 12th September 1966. The relentless programme of closures continued with passenger services being withdrawn from Monday 6th March 1967 on the railway between Cambridge,

Haverhill, Long Melford and Sudbury, leaving Long Melford with its many nearby tourist attractions without rail links. The railway south of Long Melford between Sudbury, Bures and Marks Tey was spared and has seen substantial investment and increasing passenger numbers in recent years. Today the Long Melford station building is in a well preserved condition and has a station name totem sign over the entrance door. It is used for residential accommodation. The "Long Melford Junction" nameboard from the signal box is preserved at Bressingham Steam Museum.

Lowestoft / Lowestoft Central

Lowestoft is the most easterly railway location in the UK and was of substantial importance with three railway engineering works, a busy main station, railway owned port and considerable goods facilities handling fish, coal, coke, wood, bricks, salt and oil. Much traffic was generated by the engineering works, the last of which officially closed in 1988. In 1957, the important sleeper depot creosoted 408,000 sleepers and had in store 450,000 sleepers and 250,000 cu. ft of crossing timbers. Over 2,800 tons of chairs, 340 tons of chair screws and 800,000 gallons of creosote were used annually at the depot, which closed in 1964. Some of those working there in the late 1950s included Inspector F. G. Reeve, Maintenance Fitter H. Culley, Creosoter Chargehand G. A. Purlant and Clerk in Charge H. Twiddy. The railway network in the town occupied large areas of land on both sides of the harbour and included some lines built on jetties in the North Sea. The port, a fleet of tugs and other service vessels were owned and operated by the railway until Monday 1st January 1963 when they passed to the Docks Board. The original station and the Lowestoft - Reedham railway were opened for goods traffic by the Norfolk Railway on Monday 3rd May 1847 with the passenger service commencing in early July. The first small station was replaced by the present building in 1855; this was built by Lucas Brothers and was a fine example of their work which includes amongst others, the Royal Albert Hall. Although much of the station remains today, it has been stripped of some of the original features. The unusual overall roof was removed in 1992 leaving the concourse open to the elements. Of the four original platforms three remain in use, the trackbed for the fourth now being part of the station car park. At one time this terminus had services to Yarmouth Beach (service withdrawn in 1953) and Yarmouth South Town (service withdrawn in 1970), Ipswich (and London) and Norwich. The Ipswich and Norwich lines remain today. For a short period, an omnibus service existed to Southwold and the GER noted in timetables that Lowestoft was the station for Kessingland, with the journey to that village being provided "with a frequent service of motors". Originally the station was known as Lowestoft, but from 1903 until 1970 it was known as Lowestoft Central. In 1970, following the closure of Lowestoft North it reverted in Lowestoft. The well known sign "British Railways Lowestoft Central" remains in situ at the time of writing (2010) on part of the station that is unused. This large enamel sign is designated under reference HRC 08/66. The station is located 8½ miles from Beccles, 23½ miles from Norwich Thorpe, and prior to the withdrawal of services, 12¼ miles from Yarmouth Beach and 10¼ miles from Yarmouth South Town. The distance to London Liverpool Street via Beccles is 117¾ miles. In 2010, Lowestoft is regarded as being open for freight traffic, one of the few locations in East Anglia still providing this facility. The motive power depot at Lowestoft (32C) closed in September 1960, but steam locomotives were seen there until 1965 in use as steam heating units for hauled stock.

The once important fish traffic ended on Thursday 27th September 1973, when the last truck of fish by-product left for Humberside for processing. Railway lines to the outer harbour shingle works and docks crossed the A12 trunk road in the vicinity of the station and sections of track can still be seen in the dock area. At the time of writing (April 2010) it is proposed by 1st East, a regeneration company set up by the government and supported by the local councils, that the land around the station be developed with changes made to the layout and the railway track cut back. Land made spare by these changes would be available for development, however, this proposal would be subject to a consultation process. Whilst many oppose any change in the existing station location, others want to see it moved or closed completely, with lines serving the town terminating at Oulton Broad and thus preventing road traffic being held up at three increasingly busy level crossings.

Lowestoft North

Lowestoft North was on the Lowestoft Central - Yarmouth railway line and located 2¼ miles from Lowestoft Central, 8 miles from Yarmouth South Town (services withdrawn in 1970), 10 miles from Yarmouth Beach (services withdrawn in 1953) and 120 miles from London Liverpool Street via Lowestoft Central and Beccles. Occupying a large spacious site, the station opened on Monday 13th

July 1903 and was situated on one of the two lines in East Anglia built by the Norfolk & Suffolk Joint Railways Committee, a joint venture by the GER and the M&GN. Being near to locations used for tented military camps and also a large naval base, Lowestoft North saw considerable use by Army and Naval personnel travelling to and from the Midlands and London by regular services or special chartered trains. In addition, passenger traffic was further boosted by the Camping Coaches that could be found in the loading dock. Goods handled at Lowestoft North were predominantly coal, bricks, wood and some sugar beet. At one time there were facilities and sidings for the storage of permanent way materials. Although adjacent to the busy A12 trunk road and mainly surrounded by housing, the long sloping station approaches remained unlit right up to closure. Staff at Lowestoft North were withdrawn by BR from Wednesday 12th September 1966, goods facilities were withdrawn from Monday 6th November 1967 and passenger services ceased after the last train from Yarmouth South Town ran on Saturday 2nd May 1970. The station site is now occupied by housing but much of the trackbed between Coke Ovens Junction, where the Yarmouth line left the line carrying Norwich, Ipswich and London services, has been retained together with the bridges and converted into the Great Eastern Linear Park, a cycle way and footpath costing over £500,000. However, Bridge No. 2424 that carried the A12 trunk road over the railway south of the station has been removed and the cutting filled in.

Lowestoft South Side / Lowestoft South Harbour Branch
An important goods only line left the Lowestoft - Beccles line at Oulton Broad South (previously known as Carlton Colville) and served two goods depots, sidings, factories, shipyards, private estate sidings and industrial premises in south Lowestoft and along the Lake Lothing waterfront. Originally intended as a passenger line, it never did carry passenger services but apparently at least one special train did travel down the line to the location of a proposed but never built station. The line opened within a year or so following the commencement of East Suffolk Railway passenger services in 1859 and was extended on at least two occasions to increase the area of south Lowestoft and Oulton Broad that the branch served. Major users included Boulton & Paul, J. W. Brooke & Co., Brooke Marine, Co-operative Wholesale Society [CWS] (from 1929), Colby Bros., Jewson's, Maconochie Bros. (until 1929), Morton's, local farmers, coal and other merchants. The South Side goods depot (known to local folk as Belvedere Road goods depot) dealt mainly with wood, salt, coal, bricks and other building materials although other goods passed through the depot yard from rail served waterfront industrial premises such as Morton's food factory and Richards Ironworks. The author well remembers visiting the depot on a number of occasions in the late 1950s to inspect and arrange collection of consignments of Norwegian spruce poles that had arrived in the town by rail. Opening around 1908, and with an entrance off Beaconsfield Road, Kirkley was the other depot in south Lowestoft. Here items handled included bricks, oil, spirit, sugar beet, sugar beet pulp, and coal. The sugar beet was sent to Fletton or Cantley for processing. By the 1950's the decline in traffic was noticeable as demand for goods to be carried by rail declined. Some of the very last trains using the branch carried steel for the Brooke Marine shipyard and oil for the Robey boilers at the CWS No. 2 factory. Closure was carried out in stages starting in January 1966 with Kirkley depot, followed by Belvedere Road depot and the remaining associated South Quay sidings in November 1967, and finally the Lake Lothing waterfront section extending to Oulton Broad in December 1972. The trackbed from Oulton Broad South junction, the depots, sidings and yards have all been built on, converted to footpaths, cycle ways or are now under roads or car parks. Apart from one bridge, a gate house and some isolated sections of track on private estates, few traces remain to prove that this goods line existed.

Marlesford
Opened by the ESR on Wednesday 1st June 1859 and operated by the ECR from that date, Marlesford was an intermediate station situated on the Wickham Market - Framlingham railway line. It was located 1¾ miles from Wickham Market and 4¾ miles from Framlingham. In addition to Marlesford, the station also served the village of Little Glemham. Now a private residence, the brick built station house is close to the A12 trunk road, where a level crossing once existed. Marlesford was closed to passengers by BR from Monday 3rd November 1952 and to goods traffic on Monday 13th July 1964. The line through Marlesford closed to goods from Monday 19th April 1965 but on Thursday 22nd April 1965, a truck declared unfit to travel and left at Marlesford by the last goods train on Thursday 15th April 1965, was picked up by the Leiston goods. For the last few years before passenger services were withdrawn, in some timetables the station is shown as being unstaffed with tickets and information being supplied on the train.

Mellis

Mellis was once a junction station with railway lines running north to Norwich, south to Ipswich and east to Eye. The Eye line opened in April 1867 and was closed to passengers by the LNER from Monday 2nd February 1931 and to goods traffic by BR from Monday 13th July 1964. The main line through Mellis was opened by the EUR to goods traffic on Monday 28th May 1849 and to passengers on Monday 2nd July the same year. Mellis was located 23½ miles from Norwich Thorpe, 22¾ miles from Ipswich and 91½ miles from London Liverpool Street. The line to Norwich opened in late 1849 and initially the terminus there for passenger trains stopping at or passing through Mellis was Victoria station, however within a few years they used Thorpe station. Mellis was closed by BR from Monday 28th December 1964 to goods traffic, and from Monday 7th November 1966 to passengers. During the war with Egypt and the petrol rationing in 1957, the Suffolk Hunt chartered a train to take the hounds, horses, huntsmen and followers from Bury St. Edmunds to Mellis. The train left Bury at 0930hrs and was hauled by immaculately turned out D16/3 4-4-0 No. 62615. The Hunt was picked up later at Elmswell and returned to Bury St. Edmunds. Mellis station building was demolished in the mid 1970s.

Melton

This intermediate station is on the Ipswich - Lowestoft railway line and was opened by the ESR on Wednesday 1st June 1859 and operated by the ECR from the date. The station was closed by BR to passengers from Monday 2nd May 1955 but was reopened on Monday 3rd September 1984 after a successful campaign by local railway users. Melton is 11½ miles from Ipswich, 37½ miles from Lowestoft and 80¼ miles from London Liverpool Street. Before the 1959 closure of the Beccles - Yarmouth South Town line, the distance to South Town was 41½ miles. Extensive sidings existed at Melton handling large quantities of stone and coal, and at one time a privately owned diesel shunter was based there. Goods traffic ceased to be handled from Thursday 1st June 1972 although private sidings existed after that date.

Mendlesham (Mid Suffolk Light Railway)

This intermediate station was located 4½ miles from Haughley and 14½ miles from Laxfield on the light railway that ran between these two stations. Mendlesham opened to goods traffic on Tuesday 20th September 1904 and to passengers on Tuesday 29th September 1908.

Mendlesham station shortly after the opening of the MSLR with Hudswell, Clark & Co. 0-6-0T No. 2 arriving with a Laxfield train. Under the LNER, No. 2 became Class J64 No. 8317 and was withdrawn from service in December 1929.

The station building at Mendlesham was on the down side of the main MSLR line and consisted of a timber frame clad with corrugated iron. The final passenger train ran on Saturday 26th July 1952 after which the line was closed by BR.

Mildenhall

This small medieval market town with a large military airbase nearby was the terminus of the 20¾ mile long railway from Cambridge via Fordham. The station was opened by the GER on Saturday 1st April 1885 and closed to passengers by BR from Monday 18th June 1962. Goods traffic continued to be handled at Mildenhall until Monday 13th July 1964 when the line between Fordham and Mildenhall closed. The station was 78¾ miles from London Kings Cross and 76½ miles from London Liverpool Street, both via Cambridge. A turntable existed at Mildenhall close to the signal box; this still existed when the passenger service was withdrawn in 1962. During the last years of steam operation on the Mildenhall line, the locomotives used included elderly GER designed Classes E4 and J15, and more modern LMS designed Class 2MT locomotives, these being replaced by four wheel diesel railbuses for

for the final years. The station building at Mildenhall station exists today as a private residence.

Needham / Needham Market

The intermediate station of Needham Market is on the railway line that initially carried services between Ipswich and Bury St. Edmunds, but from late 1849, has also handled services between Ipswich and Norwich (initially Norwich Victoria but later to Norwich Thorpe). Needham Market was opened as Needham by the Ipswich, Bury and Norwich Railway (IB&NR) to goods on Monday 30th November 1846 and to passengers on Thursday 24th December 1846. The official opening of the line through the uncompleted station was Monday 7th December 1846. Closed by BR from Monday 2nd January 1967, the station reopened as unstaffed Needham Market on Monday 6th December 1971. Goods traffic ceased to be handled from Monday 18th April 1966, however a private goods siding remained open after that date. In recent years, passenger services stopping at Needham Market have tended to be those on the cross country route between Cambridge/Ely and Ipswich and not between Norwich and London Liverpool Street. The station is located 8¼ miles from Ipswich, 38 miles from Norwich, 18¼ miles from Bury St. Edmunds, 47¼ miles from Cambridge and 77 miles from London Liverpool Street.

Newmarket

The first station in the town was opened to goods traffic on Monday 3rd January 1848 and to passengers on Tuesday 4th April 1848 by the Newmarket & Chesterford Railway (later changed to Newmarket Railway), the station being a terminus serving the 18 mile long line to Great Chesterford and thereby providing services to London Shoreditch (First Class fare 15/-). The railway closed from Sunday 30th June 1850 due to financial difficulties and reopened on Monday 9th September 1850 following various agreements with the ECR. The Chesterford route closed in October 1851, when a new line to Cambridge was opened using part of the old trackbed to Chesterford, plus a new section from Six Mile Bottom to Cambridge. The stations at Bourne Bridge and Balsham Road on the Chesterford route were closed. Opening in April 1854, the line from Bury St. Edmunds Northgate used the station although reversal was required to access the platform. This new route had involved constructing a tunnel of 1099 yards at Warren Hill, north of Newmarket station. The station had an island platform added in September 1879 when the Ely line opened, the two platforms being linked by a footbridge. Due to the vast amount of equine and general traffic using the railway it became obvious that the original station was struggling to cope and in April 1902, the GER opened a new larger through station complete with an oak panelled booking hall a short distance south from the first. The main part of this second station exists today having been disposed of by the railway authority and is used for offices by the owner. The first station continued in use for many years for traffic associated with horse racing and until April 1967 for goods traffic.

Shunting horses Charlie (left) and Butch (right) at Newmarket in the early 1960s. With Charlie is Lawrence Kelly, and with Butch is Horse Loading Foreman Bill Hulyer.

This fine ornate building, complete with many unusual historic features was later demolished, much to the dismay of some local residents, the site having been acquired for residential development. Including the present one, Newmarket has had four railway stations with the opening of these stations generally following the growth and decline in the use of the railway by the town's horse racing industry. The present intermediate single platform station is close to the 1902 station with accommodation for passengers provided by bus-stop type shelters. It is on the Bury St. Edmunds - Cambridge railway line and is situated 14½ miles from both Bury St. Edmunds and Cambridge, 41 miles from Ipswich, and prior to closure of the direct line, 13½ miles to Ely. Newmarket once had an engine shed, turntable, pits and full locomotive servicing facilities which were used for locomotives off the special express workings for race goers in addition to local requirements. For many years the station was well used by the horse racing industry and typically in 1962 received 748 horses and sent out 1,182. According to British Railways records the station was the last user of horses with Charlie and Butch still employed on shunting wagons and horse boxes in the 1960s. In addition to horse racing traffic, shop goods and coal, local caravan manufacture meant a large number of items such as fibre glass, aluminium and steel arrived in the town by rail with completed caravans leaving by rail, often destined for markets overseas. Steel was also received at Newmarket for the manufacture of agricultural implements. Prior to the closure of many of the nation's coal mines and subsequent reduction in the work force, large numbers of miner's helmets were dispatched from the station. In addition to Station Master C. E. Tolliday, staff at Newmarket in the early 1960s included Bill Hulyer, Lawrence Kelly, Wilfred Goult and Joyce Bradshaw. The station became unstaffed from Monday 2nd January 1967 and closed to goods traffic from Monday 3rd April 1967.

Newmarket Warren Hill

Opened by the GER in April 1885 , this station was located at the north end of Warren Hill tunnel and close to the railway triangle that existed until the 1960s giving direct access to Bury St. Edmunds as now, and also to Ely. Warren Hill station served the locality, race goers and the horse racing industry. It was convenient for those arriving at Newmarket from cities such as Lincoln, Leeds and Manchester on special trains to attend the races. The station was closed by the LNER in 1939.

Orwell

This intermediate station was one of the original stations opened by the Felixstowe Railway and Pier Company (FR&PC) on Tuesday 1st May 1877. Orwell was on the Westerfield - Felixstowe railway line and served the villages of Bucklesham and Nacton. It was used by the FR&PC founder Colonel George Tomline, who lived at nearby Orwell Park. Orwell was closed to passenger and goods traffic from Monday 15th June 1959 and had been located 9¼ miles from Ipswich, 9 miles from Felixstowe Pier, 8 miles from Felixstowe Beach and 6½ miles from Felixstowe Town (GER mileages, those of the LNER/BR may differ slightly).

Mutford / Oulton Broad (Mutford) / Oulton Broad / Oulton Broad North

This intermediate station is on the Lowestoft - Norwich railway line and adjacent to Oulton Broad North Junction where the track carrying services to Ipswich diverges from that carrying Norwich services. In the past, rail access to a shipyard and a fuel depot existed near the junction. Both shipyard and fuel depot closed many years ago and little evidence exists of these rail connections. Oulton Broad North is a busy station located 1½ miles from Lowestoft and 22 miles from Norwich. At one time, until they were withdrawn in the mid 1930s, services between Yarmouth South Town and Lowestoft Central via St. Olaves stopped here, the distance to Yarmouth South Town being 13 miles. The present station was not the first to serve the locality; this was a short distance further west and on the Norwich side of the A1117 level crossing. This crossing has been the subject of much correspondence in local newspapers from road users complaining about delays caused by trains. The first station at this location was operated by the Norfolk Railway and opened for goods in May 1847 and passengers the following July. It was known as Mutford and in July 1881, was renamed Oulton Broad (Mutford). The present station opened with the doubling of the original line in 1904 and was originally Oulton Broad (Mutford) becoming Oulton Broad in 1915. On Monday 26th September 1927, the station was again renamed when it became Oulton Broad North. The goods service was withdrawn from Monday 13th July 1964, however a private siding existed after that date. Like many others in the area, Oulton Broad North became unstaffed from Monday 6th March 1967. The buildings on the up platform have been demolished and replaced by bus-stop type shelters, but those on the down platform still exist and are in use as an Indian restaurant, the original canopy providing some shelter to passengers.

Carlton Colville / Oulton Broad South

Oulton Broad South is an intermediate station on the Ipswich - Lowestoft railway line and until 1972 was the location of the junction for the goods only line to South Lowestoft. The station was opened on Wednesday 1st June 1859 by the ESR and operated by the ECR from that date. Oulton Broad South was known as Carlton Colville until Monday 26th September 1927, and is located 2 miles from Lowestoft Central, 6½ miles from Beccles, 47 miles from Ipswich and 115¾ miles from London Liverpool Street. Camping Coaches were for many years a feature of the station;

these were to be found in a siding adjacent to the down platform. The goods service was withdrawn from Monday 13th July 1964, and the station became unstaffed from Monday 6th March 1967.

Camping Coach No. 122 at Oulton Broad South in the 1950s.

Following the modernisation and introduction of new signalling on the East Suffolk line in the mid 1980s, this station is now situated on a single track section of this important line and uses the former up platform. The main station building exists in non railway use and the canopy has been retained and provides shelter for passengers. The down platform is partly dismantled but the original building exists, and has been converted to a hairdressing salon.

Parham / Parham Halt

Opened by the ESR on Wednesday 1st June 1859 and operated by the ECR from that date, Parham was an intermediate station on the Wickham Market - Framlingham railway line. Located 4 miles from Wickham Market, 2½ miles from Framlingham and 88½ miles from London Liverpool Street, Parham was busiest during World War II when it received large quantities of munitions and fuel for the nearby American air base. The station was closed to passengers by BR from Monday 3rd November 1952 and to goods traffic from Monday 13th July 1964. The traditional brick station building still exists and is now incorporated in a large residential property. Parham was shown in timetables as a Halt for the last few years before passenger services were withdrawn, with tickets and information being supplied on the train.

Raydon / Raydon Wood

Raydon was formally opened on Friday 20th August 1847 by the Eastern Union & Hadleigh Junction Railway. The goods service commenced the following day, and the first passenger train ran on Thursday 2nd September 1847. Located on the Bentley - Hadleigh railway line, this intermediate station was situated 5 miles from Bentley, 2¼ miles from Hadleigh, and 68¼ miles from London Liverpool Street. In October 1895, Raydon was renamed Raydon Wood. The station was closed to passengers by the LNER from Monday 29th February 1932, but retained a goods service until Monday 19th April 1965 when the line was closed by BR. After the withdrawal of the passenger service, the signal box was privately purchased and moved from Raydon Wood to a builder's yard at Capel St. Mary. On Wednesday 25th February 1998, it was moved to Bressingham Steam Museum where it is to be restored to working order using equipment from Oakington signal box. The Museum received a 50% grant from National Museum of Science & Industry PRISM Fund to purchase the signal box, which according to information on display at Bressingham was built by the GER in 1894.

Saxham and Risby

Saxham and Risby was an intermediate station on the Bury St. Edmunds Northgate - Newmarket railway line, and served the villages of Little Saxby, Risby All Saints and Great Saxham. It opened on Saturday 1st April 1854 having been built by the Newmarket & Chesterford Railway and was operated from the outset by the ECR. Saxham and Risby was located 3 miles from Bury St. Edmunds, 29½ miles from Ipswich, 26 miles from Cambridge and 25 miles from Ely. Goods traffic ceased to be handled at Saxham and Risby from Monday 28th December 1964, although a private siding existed after that date. Passenger services were withdrawn from Monday 2nd January 1967. The station was demolished and little evidence remains that it ever existed.

Saxmundham Spa / Saxmundham

Saxmundham is on the Ipswich - Lowestoft railway line and was once a junction station with railway lines running north to Beccles, Lowestoft and Yarmouth, south to Ipswich, and east to Leiston and Aldeburgh. Passenger services on the 8¼ mile single track railway to Aldeburgh were withdrawn in September 1966, but the line remains open from Saxmundham Junction, approximate ½ mile north of the station, to Sizewell siding for the nearby French operated nuclear power station. Saxmundham is located 22¼ miles from Ipswich, 18¼ miles from Beccles and 91 miles from London Liverpool Street. Prior to the 1959 closure of the direct line between Beccles and Yarmouth South Town, Saxmundham was 30¾ miles from Yarmouth. The station had three platforms but the bay platform has been filled in and is now outside the railway boundary. However, Saxmundham does still retain a siding, an unusual feature for stations between Oulton Broad South and Westerfield. The station had staggered platforms with the down platform buildings between two level crossings. This platform had a moveable section that allowed it to be extended across one of the roads thereby forming a long continuous platform. When not required for rail passengers, the moveable section was swung to one side to open the road for traffic, and formed a level crossing. After 1980 when a new down platform was built opposite the existing up platform, the old down platform and buildings were removed. The station, shown on some early railway maps as "Saxmundham Spa", was opened by the ESR on Wednesday 1st June 1859 and operated by the ECR from that date. It closed to goods traffic from Monday 19th April 1965 and became unstaffed from Monday 6th March 1967. At the time of writing, the former signal box on the down platform serves as a communications centre for the East Suffolk Line and the line to Sizewell.

Seven Hills Halt

One of a number of intermediate halts opened in late 1922 by the GER, Seven Hills Halt was between Barnham and Ingham on the Bury St. Edmunds - Thetford railway line. The halt was located 5¾ miles from Bury St. Edmunds and 7 miles from Thetford. Passengers to and from Seven Hills Halt were required to join, or alight from, the special carriage provided. A private goods siding existed at this location. Seven Hills Halt was closed to goods traffic by the GER from Wednesday 1st May 1918 and by BR to passengers from Monday 8th June 1953.

Sizewell

A general goods siding existed at Sizewell and this closed from Sunday 6th March 1966. Complete with heavy lifting gantry, the present siding is used for traffic associated with the nearby French operated nuclear power station. It is located approximately 1 mile south east of the site of Leiston station, the line originally having been built by the ESR in 1860 as part of the Aldeburgh extension from Leiston.

Snape / Snape Bridge

Snape was opened by the ESR on Wednesday 1st June 1859 and operated by the ECR from that date. It was the terminus of a short single track goods only line from Snape Junction (between Wickham Market and Saxmundham) that served the goods yard and maltings at Snape. A number of private lines and sidings existed within the maltings complex and on the quay. Intended at one time as a passenger line, the 1½ mile long line was visited by at least one special passenger train organised primarily for railway enthusiasts, and was closed by BR from Monday 7th March 1960.

Somerleyton

This intermediate station is on the Lowestoft - Norwich railway line and close to the Norfolk/Suffolk border. At one time, until the service was withdrawn in the mid 1930s, Somerleyton was a station for services between Yarmouth South Town and Lowestoft Central via St. Olaves, the distance to Yarmouth South Town being 9 miles. The line passing through the station was opened by the Norfolk Railway for goods from Monday 3rd May 1847 and passengers the following July, having been built by the Lowestoft Railway and Harbour Company. Somerleyton is located 5½ miles from Lowestoft and 18 miles from Norwich and closed to goods traffic from Monday 13th July 1964. The station has been unstaffed since Monday 6th March 1967.

Southwold (Southwold Railway [narrow gauge])

This station formed the coastal terminus of the 9 mile long 3ft. narrow gauge railway from Halesworth. By changing trains at Halesworth, Southwold was 109¾ miles from London Liverpool Street. The station opened in Wednesday 24th September 1879 and closed to passengers from Friday 12th April 1929. In addition to sidings, at Southwold there was an engine shed and after 1902, a carriage shed. The last steaming of a locomotive on the railway took place on 20th April 1929. A one mile long goods only line was constructed to Southwold harbour and Blackshore Quay in 1914. This left the "main" line between Walberswick and Southwold just north of the bridge that carried the railway across the River Blyth. At the harbour, in addition to sidings and a run round loop, a shed and weighbridge were constructed.

Stoke / Stoke (Suffolk)
This intermediate station was on the Cambridge - Haverhill - Long Melford railway line and was opened by the GER on Wednesday 9th August 1865. Stoke served the village of Stoke by Clare and was located 8½ miles from Long Melford, 5 miles from Haverhill, 23¼ miles from Cambridge and 28¼ miles from Colchester via Marks Tey. The station closed to goods traffic from Monday 19th April 1965, became unstaffed from 28th January 1963 and closed to passengers from Monday 6th March 1967. In June 1932, Stoke was renamed Stoke (Suffolk) reverting back to Stoke in June 1965. The station has been converted to a private residence with an extension, and the track bed has been filled in to approximately platform height. A bridge adjacent to the station which once carried the A1092 road over the railway has been removed.

Stowmarket
The official opening of the line through Stowmarket by the Ipswich, Bury and Norwich Railway (IB&NR) took place on Monday 7th December 1846. However, the station opened to goods on Monday 30th November 1846 and to passengers on Thursday 24th December 1846, shortly before the IB&NR and the EUR amalgamated. Initially carrying services between Ipswich and Bury St. Edmunds, from late 1849, it also handled services between Ipswich and Norwich (originally Norwich Victoria but later to Norwich Thorpe). The station is located 80¾ miles from London Liverpool Street, 34½ miles from Norwich (Thorpe), 12 miles from Ipswich and 14¼ miles from Bury St. Edmunds. Designed by Frederick Barnes, Stowmarket station buildings have been the subject of a restoration project carried out by British Rail and the Railway Heritage Trust, the work being completed in May 1987. There has been a number of important industrial concerns in the town, some of which were rail connected. These include the Cordite Works and more recently the large ICI factory. Stowmarket was a sub shed of Ipswich (32B) and a small steam or diesel locomotive was usually stabled there for shunting in the yard, and on occasion at Needham. Recently the yard has been used for the stabling of track maintenance vehicles and diesel locomotives belonging to Direct Rail Services, a company employed on Rail Head Treatment Trains and special duties. This company has an office at the station.

Stradbroke (Mid Suffolk Light Railway)
This intermediate station was located 15 miles from Haughley and 4 miles from Laxfield on the light railway that ran between these two stations. The timber frame and corrugated iron clad station building was on the up side of the main MSLR line. Stradbroke opened to goods traffic on Tuesday 20th September 1904 and passengers four years later, on Tuesday 29th September 1908. The final passenger train left the station on Saturday 26th July 1952 after which the line was closed by BR.

Sudbury / Sudbury (Suffolk)
Built by the Colchester, Stour Valley, Sudbury & Halstead Railway, this line formally opened on Wednesday 11th July 1849 although it had actually opened the previous week. The railway was leased to the Ipswich, Bury and Norwich Railway (IB&NR) which later amalgamated with the EUR. Sudbury was the original terminus of the line from Marks Tey and became an intermediate station in August 1865, when the railway was extended north to Long Melford, and from there west to Haverhill and north to Bury St. Edmunds. The original 1849 terminus station was replaced at that time but remained in railway use, being demolished much later. The name of the station was changed from Sudbury to Sudbury (Suffolk) in June 1932 but reverted to Sudbury on Monday 14th June 1965. A small engine shed existed at Sudbury which was a sub shed of Ipswich, this had locomotive servicing facilities and closed in the late 1950s. The station became unstaffed from Monday 15th August 1966 and goods traffic ceased to be handled at Sudbury from Monday 31st October 1966. In 1967, the station regained terminus status when the line north of the town closed. The 1865 station was demolished and replaced in October 1990 by a new platform and waiting shelter situated close by. Sudbury is located 11¾ miles from Marks Tey, 58½ miles from London Liverpool Street and 16¾ miles from Colchester. The station was 34¾ miles from Cambridge prior to the closure of the Cambridge - Haverhill - Long Melford - Sudbury route. The station has received numerous awards for the volunteer maintained station garden.

Thorpeness / Thorpeness Halt
Thorpeness was an intermediate station set in an idyllic heathland location quite close to the beach on the Saxmundham - Aldeburgh railway line. It was located 6¼ miles from Saxmundham, 2 miles from Aldeburgh and 97¼ miles from London Liverpool Street. The station was opened by the GER in July 1914 and closed by BR after the last train ran on Saturday 10th September 1966. However a special train for Thorpeness Golf Club was run on Saturday 17th September. Goods traffic had ceased to be handled at Thorpeness

from Monday 30th November 1959 and the station was unstaffed from Monday 18th June 1962. Shelter for passengers was provided by using grounded carriage bodies positioned at the rear of the platform. Remains of the platform and the carriage body supports can still be seen in the extensively wooded undergrowth. This station was very popular with visitors to the nearby hotel, golf course and the unique village resort of Thorpeness, which includes a large artificial lake known as the "Meare".

Thurston

The intermediate station at Thurston is on the busy east/west cross country railway line carrying services between Peterborough, Ely, Cambridge, Newmarket, Bury St. Edmunds and Ipswich. The official opening of the line by the Ipswich, Bury and Norwich Railway (IB&NR) through the uncompleted station was Monday 7th December 1846, however, Thurston opened to goods on Monday 30th November 1846 and to passengers on Thursday 24th December 1846, shortly before the IB&NR and the EUR amalgamated. The station is located 4¼ miles from Bury St. Edmunds, 22¼ miles from Ipswich, 33¼ miles from Cambridge and 32¼ miles from Ely. The buildings on the up platform were demolished in the mid 1960s and replaced by a bus-stop type shelter but the unusual three storey building on the down platform still exists but not in railway use, the canopy providing shelter for passengers. Thurston closed to goods traffic from Tuesday 1st June 1976 and the sidings were recovered shortly afterwards. At one time a substantial granary existed at Thurston which was rail connected, but the sidings were last used for deliveries of coal.

Trimley

Trimley was not one of the original stations established by the Felixstowe Railway and Pier Company when the line between Westerfield and Felixstowe Pier opened in 1877, but was opened by the GER on Friday 1st May 1891. Prior to becoming unstaffed from Monday 12th September 1966, Trimley regularly won prizes in the station gardens competition for the fine floral and topiary displays. In the last years before becoming unstaffed, the staff at Trimley included Porters D.C. Dickerson and A. Illum, and in the signal box on the up platform, Signalman J. Smith could usually be found. The station remains open to passengers but was closed by BR to goods traffic from Monday 13th July 1964. Trimley is located 10½ miles from Westerfield, 1¾ miles from Felixstowe (Town), 14 miles from Ipswich and 82¾ miles from London Liverpool Street.

On the Ipswich side of the Station Road level crossing at Trimley, a junction exists that gives access to one of the two railway lines to the Felixstowe Dock and Railway Company (FD&RC) estate. The down platform at Trimley remains in use, but both tracks through the station are used. In the late 1980s, the former up loop line at the Felixstowe end of the station was diverted and extended over a mile to the North Container Terminal, leaving the down line for passenger services to Felixstowe and traffic for the South Container Terminal. It is planned by the FD&RC to lay an additional railway line of 7150 metres (almost 4½ miles) in length from Trimley towards Ipswich as part of the planned improvements to the rail access to the Port of Felixstowe. At the time of writing, Suffolk Coastal District Council is attempting to prevent Network Rail demolishing Trimley station building by requesting the government to list it as being of special architectural or historic interest. The request was made on Friday 6th February 2009 and was valid for six months during which time Network Rail could not start demolition. In October 2009, the Victorian Society joined the campaign to save the station.

Walberswick (Southwold Railway [narrow gauge])

Walberswick was an intermediate station on the 3ft. gauge Southwold Railway that ran between Halesworth and Southwold. The station opened after the opening of the railway, with the Board of Trade recording it as being on Saturday 1st July 1882. It was located 8 miles from Halesworth and 1 mile from Southwold and closed from Monday 2nd April 1917, reopened following the end of hostilities, and closed from Friday 12th April 1929 with the closure of the railway.

Welnetham

Opened by the GER on Wednesday 9th August 1865, Welnetham was an intermediate station on the Bury St. Edmunds Northgate - Long Melford railway line. The station was located 5 miles from Bury St. Edmunds, 11½ miles from Long Melford, 26¼ miles from Marks Tey and 73 miles from London Liverpool Street. Welnetham was closed by BR to passengers from Monday 10th April 1961, and to goods traffic from Monday 13th July 1964. Despite being closed to passengers, Welnetham did appear in the British Railways timetable for the period 12th June to 10th September 1961 with passengers being advised that the locality was served by omnibuses. The station building exists and has been converted and extended to serve as a private residence.

Wenhaston (Southwold Railway [narrow gauge])
Wenhaston was an intermediate station on the 3ft. gauge Southwold Railway that ran between Halesworth and Southwold. It opened with the railway on Wednesday 24th September 1879, and the siding at Wenhaston Mill opened in November 1880. The first winter (1879) timetable issued by the railway stated that trains stopped at Wenhaston by hand signal only and passengers wishing to alight there must inform the Guard at the starting station. The station was located 2½ miles from Halesworth and 6½ miles from Southwold, and closed from Friday 12th April 1929 with the railway.

Westerfield
The first railway at Westerfield was built by the EUR, opened with the ESR on Wednesday 1st June 1859, and operated by the ECR from that date. The Westerfield terminus of the Felixstowe Railway and Pier Company (FR&PC) line was constructed adjacent to the up platform of the original station and opened on Tuesday 1st May 1877. This is now a private residence having been sold by BR in the 1980s. The FR&PC was operated by the GER from Monday 1st September 1879 and purchased by them on Tuesday 5th July 1887. Under GER control, the FR&PC station was closed with Felixstowe trains working through to Ipswich and passengers no longer having to change trains at Westerfield. In addition to Felixstowe passenger services and those on the East Suffolk line to Lowestoft, today a vast quantity of rail borne containers and other goods pass through Westerfield going to and from Felixstowe. In addition, there can be the occasional train serving Sizewell Power Station passing through the station. One event which the station is noted for in railway history took place at 8.43am on Tuesday 25th September 1900, when the boiler of GER Class Y14 0-6-0 No. 522 exploded, killing Driver John Barnard and Fireman William MacDonald. Both men received extensive burns and injuries and their bodies were thrown considerable distances by the force of the explosion. The 1899 built engine was wrecked, but was rebuilt and returned to service with a new boiler. It had been shunting in the up side sidings when the incident occurred. In 1901, it was intended to construct a railway from Westerfield to Kenton on the Mid Suffolk Light Railway; however despite a ceremony in 1902 to officially start the construction, the line was never built. In addition to sidings at the station, at one time a railway line extended from Westerfield to a nearby brick and tile works. This junction station became unstaffed from Monday 6th March 1967 and closed to goods traffic from Monday 13th July 1964. Westerfield is located 3¾ miles from Ipswich, 45½ miles from Lowestoft, 12¼ miles from Felixstowe (Town) and 72½ miles from London Liverpool Street.

Wickham Market
Now an intermediate station between Saxmundham and Melton stations on the Ipswich - Lowestoft line, Wickham Market was at one time a junction station for the 6½ mile single track line to the historic town of Framlingham. The junction was approximately 1 mile north of the station where a bay platform was used by the Framlingham trains. Passenger services to Framlingham were withdrawn on Wednesday 3rd December 1952 but the line remained open to goods traffic for another 13 years. Wickham Market is located 84½ miles from London Liverpool Street, 15¾ miles from Ipswich and 33¼ miles from Lowestoft. Opened by the ESR on Wednesday 1st June 1859 and operated by the ECR from that date, the station is at Campsea Ashe and about 2 miles from the small town of Wickham Market. It was closed to goods traffic by BR from Monday 13th July 1964 and has been unstaffed from Monday 6th March 1967.

Wilby (Mid Suffolk Light Railway)
This intermediate station was located 16½ miles from Haughley and 2½ miles from Laxfield on the light railway that ran between these two stations. It was considered the least used on the line. The station building was on the down side of the main MSLR line and as with other stations on this railway, this was of timber frame construction clad with corrugated iron, but was smaller than most seen on the MSLR. A grounded van body on the platform was used as a store. Wilby opened to passengers in July 1909 and goods later that year. The final passenger train ran on Saturday 26th July 1952 after which the line was closed by BR.

Woodbridge
The busy intermediate station at Woodbridge is on the Ipswich - Lowestoft line and was built by the EUR, opened with the ESR on Wednesday 1st June 1859, and operated by the ECR from that date. Woodbridge closed to goods traffic from Monday 18th April 1966 and became unstaffed from Monday 6th March 1967. A one time notable feature of the station was the horse worked tramway from the station to Gladwell's and Sun Wharves on the River Deben. Located 10¼ miles from Ipswich, 38¾ miles from Lowestoft and 79 miles from London Liverpool Street, Woodbridge is an important

market town with the station set in an attractive waterfront location. Since 1992 part of the station building has been used as a café and also provides bed and breakfast accommodation. The former goods shed has been refurbished and is in use for retail and other purposes.

Mildenhall Golf Links Halt / Worlington Golf Links Halt
The halt was opened by the GER as Mildenhall Golf Links Halt in November 1922 and renamed Worlington Golf Links Halt by the LNER in January 1923. Situated between Mildenhall and Isleham Halt on the Cambridge - Mildenhall railway line, the halt was located 19¾ miles from Cambridge and 1 mile from Mildenhall. Passengers to and from Worlington Golf Links Halt were required to join, or alight from, the special "car" provided. Worlington Golf Links Halt was closed by BR from Monday 18th June 1962.

Worlingworth (Mid Suffolk Light Railway)
This intermediate station was located 12 miles from Haughley and 7 miles from Laxfield on the light railway that ran between these two stations. The station building was on the down side of the main MSLR line and as with others on the MSLR, this was of timber frame construction clad with corrugated iron. The railway opened to goods traffic on Tuesday 20th September 1904 but Worlingworth was not one of those stations providing a goods service at that time. Passenger services commenced at the station on Tuesday 29th September 1908. The final passenger train ran on Saturday 26th July 1952 after which the line was closed by BR.

Yaxley Halt
Located at Duke's Bridge approximately mid way between Mellis and Eye, Yaxley Halt was opened by the GER on Wednesday 20th December 1922 in the hope of attracting further passengers to the three mile long Eye - Mellis railway line. The halt was closed by the LNER from Monday 2nd February 1931, the last passenger train having run between Mellis and Eye the previous Saturday. The line remained open for goods traffic until Monday 13th July 1964 when it was closed by BR.

NOTES

BRITISH RAILWAYS (BR)
Where "British Railways" or "BR" is shown, this can represent the Railway Executive of the British Transport Commission, the British Transport Commission or the British Railways Board.

COUNTY BOUNDARIES
A few stations are located in Suffolk and the town or village they serve is in a different county and vice versa. The boundaries used are those in 2010.

DISTANCE
Distances quoted are extracted from various British Railways and Bradshaw publications and are rounded to the nearest ¼ mile. The use of miles and chains, and miles and yards, which are sometimes used in publications with regard to railway distances, was not considered suitable for this book due to the need for flexibility, completeness in stating route distances and future considerations. With imperial measure being erased from the UK and no longer taught in schools, in future people will know little of miles (and even less of chains and yards) being only familiar with the metric system where 1 kilometre = 0.62 miles (1 mile = 1.609 kilometres).

EAST SUFFOLK LINE
Since early 1986, train control on the East Suffolk Line between Oulton Broad South and Westerfield, and Saxmundham and Sizewell has been carried out by radio from the communications centre housed in the former signal box on the down platform at Saxmundham.

OWNERSHIP
The majority of the stations and railways mentioned in this book were transferred to the Great Eastern Railway (GER) in August 1862, the London and North Eastern Railway (LNER) in January 1923, and British Railways (BR) in January 1948. In 1993, the then Conservative government set about the privatisation of British Railways and as a result the network and infrastructure eventually passed to Railtrack and subsequently to Network Rail. Private companies, many with foreign (EU) holdings and others with foreign based parent companies, consequently took over the running of passenger services, goods/freight services and most stations.

FELIXSTOWE DOCK AND RAILWAY COMPANY (FD&RC)
In 1879, the Felixstowe Railway and Pier Company became the Felixstowe Railway and Dock Company following a reappraisal of the company's interests and operations. In 1887, the GER took over the Westerfield - Felixstowe railway having worked it since 1879, and the Company became the Felixstowe Dock and Railway Company. With the need to increase rail traffic to and from the Port of Felixstowe, plans have been announced to upgrade the capacity of the railway to the port. Alterations are also planned for Ipswich yard to accommodate the extra traffic and this includes the closure of the railway to the Lower Yard. For details, readers are advised to consult the following 12 page document which was issued by the Office of Public Sector Information.This order was made on 23rd September 2008 and came into force on 14th October 2008. All rail measurements in the document use the metric system:-

Statutory Instruments 2008 No. 2512
The Felixstowe Branch Line and Ipswich Yard Improvement Order 2008

LOWESTOFT RAILWAY & HARBOUR COMPANY (LR&HC)

Much published information including that found in local history books, railway books and on the internet, gives the impression that developer and contractor Samuel Morton Peto was responsible for the achievements of the LR&HC. The LR&HC was incorporated in 1845 and the Norfolk Railway empowered in 1846 to purchase, or lease in perpetuity, the LR&HC. Substantial evidence exists showing the Norfolk Railway was responsible for completing the Lowestoft to Reedham line, and that Lowestoft harbour was developed by the Norfolk, Eastern Counties and Great Eastern Railways. Directors of the LR&HC included Sir Thomas Sherlock Gooch Bt (*Chairman*), Sir Francis Holyoake Goodricke Bt, Edward Leathes, Thomas Morse, Francis Mills, Adam Duff and Charles Tyndale. No mention is made of Mr. Peto in the Act of Parliament for the LR&HC which is dated 30th June 1845.

MID SUFFOLK LIGHT RAILWAY (MSLR)

The MSLR was transferred to the LNER in mid 1924; however the transfer is officially recorded as 1st January 1923. In 1990, a project was started which led to the formation of a MSLR Museum based at a recreated Brockford station and established as far as possible using reclaimed buildings and materials from along the route of the original railway. A café, museum, shop and workshops have been established on this site, with track and sidings having been laid on the original track bed. Trains, usually steam hauled, using restored rolling stock provide rides during the operating season.

SOUTHWOLD RAILWAY (SR)

The SR was a unique narrow gauge (3ft.) railway that ran from Southwold to a terminus adjacent to the GER/LNER station at Halesworth. The line opened on Wednesday 24th September 1879, although not all stations opened at that time. Despite attempts to keep the line open, including seeking assistance from the LNER, the last passenger train ran on Thursday 11th April 1929. In 2010, the Southwold Railway Trust has plans to reopen part of the original railway at Wenhaston. Plans are also in hand to build a replica SR Sharp, Stewart 2-4-0T locomotive.

MODERNISATION AND CLOSURE

In some cases where a station has been closed, rationalised or modernised, the buildings may no longer exist, or if they do, they have been altered and bear little resemblance to when the station was staffed with full facilities. Many buildings at stations that still provide passenger services have been demolished and replaced by bus-stop type shelters or similar for passengers' use, an example being Sudbury. With development, redevelopment and regeneration schemes common in many Suffolk towns and villages, it is often the case that any signs of the railway have been completely erased making it impossible to find any trace of an old track bed or station, an example of this being Bungay. For this reason, preference in this book has been given to photographs over maps which may have little or no resemblance to the present day landscape whereas photographs often do. Having been sold by the railway authorities, many well preserved former station buildings exist such as those at Clare and Marlesford.

OTHER RAILWAYS

Several leisure activity narrow gauge and miniature railways have existed in Suffolk, some of which still operate. These include the 2ft. gauge East Suffolk Light Railway that opened in 1973 and forms part of the East Anglia Transport Museum. Pleasurewood Hills has a substantial 2ft. gauge railway used for transporting visitors around the park and a smaller miniature railway for pleasure rides. Steam worked miniature railways of the past include those at Felixstowe, Lowestoft, Kessingland and Somerleyton.

UNSTAFFED STATIONS

Apart from Bury St. Edmunds, Ipswich, Lowestoft and Stowmarket, those stations still open by the late 1960s were unstaffed with passenger enquires being answered and fares collected on the train.

Lowestoft Sleeper Depot was constructed in 1914 on essentially what were mud flats and covered 15 acres. Vessels from the Baltic and other European countries discharged wood at the 1000ft. quay directly on to internal yard wagons. Supplies also came from London and Immingham Docks by rail to Lowestoft. One of the steam cranes at the depot is seen here in the process of stacking sleepers. In addition to the cranes, the depot was home to Sentinel Class Y1 and Y3 locomotives. Lowestoft served the southern portion of the Eastern Region with up to three trains each day leaving the depot with processed sleepers and other products. *Courtesy Peter Calvert*

A SELECTION OF SUFFOLK RAILWAY SCENES IN COLOUR

The signal box at Cavendish makes a splendid sight in the late afternoon sun with even the fire buckets shining in this view recorded in 1964. However, like the railway it served, it is now just a distant memory. Other photographs of Cavendish featured elsewhere in this book originated from the last signalman at Cavendish, Mr. Bernard Saunders.
Copyright Stuart Jones

Complete with the British Rail large logo on the body side, Class 47/4 Co-Co No. 47526 *Northumbria* waits to depart from platform four at Ipswich with the 1630hrs London Liverpool Street - Norwich service on Sunday 5th April 1987. The Class 47 diesel electric locomotives were built by Brush Traction and first introduced in 1963. They are powered by a Sulzer 12LDA28C diesel engine developing 2580bhp with electrical equipment supplied by the builder. The locomotive seen here was withdrawn from service in June 1998.
Copyright Malcolm R. White

A once very busy station in terms of goods traffic, livestock and passenger numbers, Newmarket has seen a drastic reduction in railway business and infrastructure. Photographs of the first station, which opened in 1848 as a terminus and was enlarged as a through station in 1879, can be found elsewhere in this book. A new larger station south of the old site opened in April 1902 and this replaced the original station. Referred to by many as the "new" station, this has been replaced by a modern basic station, built close by, and it is this that serves Newmarket today. Parts of the 1902 station still exist but have been disposed of by the railway authorities.

Top - This external view shows the station in 1905 when almost new. It is this building that exists but not in railway use.

Bottom - A comprehensive view in 1906 of the through platforms of the 1902 station.
Both Malcolm R. White Collection

At the time of writing (2010), the future of Lowestoft station, the most easterly in the British Isles, is uncertain. These scenes show the interior of the station before the overall roof was removed in 1992. **Top Left** - The polished buffers and lamps were a well known feature of the station. Unfortunately, they no longer receive the care and attention they did when this view was recorded on New Years Day 1986. **Top Right** - The station clock and the arches through which the telephone kiosk, ticket office and ladies waiting room were situated. **Bottom Left** - Recorded on Sunday 15th December 1985, this view is looking across the concourse with a diesel multiple unit in platform four. The bookstall, dog's bowl, chocolate machines and Christmas Tree can be seen. The gentlemen's toilets were to the left of the bookstall, and the wooden tables seen to the right of the bookstall, were used to sort newspapers out that arrived early each morning by the newspaper train and also to display goods.

All photographs copyright Norman Fairhead

A fine view of Class B1 4-6-0 No. 61233 arriving at Lowestoft with an express from London Liverpool Street in June 1957. This locomotive was one of the seventeen of the class used as steam heating units in the early 1960s and in 1963 became Departmental Locomotive No. 21. It was scrapped in 1966. Much of the infrastructure seen here no longer exists including Coke Ovens signal box in the top left, the covered loading platforms on the left and Lowestoft locomotive shed in the distance. One of the 2-4-2T locomotives designed by S.D. Holden for the Great Eastern Railway, of which a number were allocated to Lowestoft, is seen heading for the station.
Copyright Colour Rail / E.. Alger.

On Monday 1st August 1977, Class 100 diesel multiple unit No. E11115 stands in platform three at Lowestoft. The station concourse at that time had an overall roof and this can be seen in the background. Class 100 diesel multiple units were introduced in 1957 having been built by the Gloucester Railway Carriage & Wagon Company. Four examples have been preserved.
Copyright Malcolm R. White

The area previously occupied by the station, goods shed and yard at Lavenham is now an industrial estate, but in June 1959 when this scene was recorded, it was an important part of the transport infrastructure of this historic town. This classic scene shows Class J15 0-6-0 No. 65457 entering Lavenham with a passenger train from Bury St. Edmunds. Nothing remains of this attractive station.
Copyright Colour Rail / J. R. Besley

Class E4 2-4-0 No. 62797 heading a south bound train possibly to Colchester, pauses at the junction station of Long Melford. Completed in August 1902 as GER Class T26 No. 1259, No. 62797 was condemned in March 1958. Other numbers carried by this locomotive include GER No. 416 (in 1920), LNER No. 7416 (in 1926), LNER No. 7796 (in 1942), and LNER No. 2797 (in 1946). A type usually found in East Anglia, this locomotive was allocated to sheds in North East England between 1935 and 1941. Following the closure of the railway through Long Melford, the former station building and platform now serves as a private residence.
Copyright Colour Rail / N. Sprinks

An overall view of Stoke station looking east with Class D16/3 4-4-0 No. 62510 entering the station with a Cambridge train. Completed in 1900 as GER Class S46 4-4-0 No. 1899, No. 62510 was withdrawn in October 1957. It was built and scrapped at Stratford.
Copyright Colour Rail / D. T. Cobbe

A charming 1950s view of a rural Suffolk railway with Class J15 0-6-0 No. 65457 arriving at Cockfield station with a train from Bury St. Edmunds. The bridge under which the train has passed exists today, but the opening has been closed with a grass bank. In late 2009, the station building and platform both existed but in a derelict condition. Closed to passengers in April 1961, special charter passenger trains passed through the station in June 1962.
Copyright Colour Rail / E. Alger

Now part of the national collection and at the time of writing on display at Bressingham Steam Museum, Class E4 2-4-0 No. 62785 is seen here at Mildenhall in May 1958 waiting to leave with a passenger train for Cambridge.
Copyright Colour Rail / J. G. Dewing

A fine view of Oulton Broad Swing Bridge on the East Suffolk line in the 1950s, with a Lowestoft Central - London Liverpool Street express crossing headed by a Class B1 4-6-0 locomotive. At the time this scene was recorded the bridge was double track, but in 1985 it was reduced to single track as part of the East Suffolk line modernisation and resignalling scheme. This steam scene has been recreated in recent years when four railtours hauled by four different locomotives have visited Lowestoft. The nearest station to this bridge on the East Suffolk line is Oulton Broad South.
Copyright Colour Rail / E. Alger

An interesting summer scene at Beccles in the 1950s with a London bound express arriving from the coast hauled by an almost new Brush Type 2 A1A-A1A (later Class 31) No. D5506. Many aspects of Beccles no longer seen are in this comprehensive view including the Waveney Valley line to Tivetshall passing behind the signal box in the top left, all the platforms including the bay in use and the fine water crane at the platform end. Several passengers, in fashionable 1950s clothes, are waiting for a down train.
Copyright Colour Rail / E..Alger

At Marlesford, the A12 trunk road crossed the railway that ran between Wickham Market and Framlingham and on the left of this photograph, the level crossing gates for this road crossing can be seen. Ipswich based Class 15 Bo-Bo diesel locomotive No. D8215 is seen here at Marlesford with a goods train consisting of coal wagons. D8215 was scrapped at Crewe in November 1971.
Copyright Colour Rail

On Good Friday 12th April 1963, the stock of a rambler's excursion is propelled out of Framlingham platform by Class 31/1 A1A-A1A No. D5595. This locomotive was later renumbered 31175 and was scrapped at Carlisle in July 1988, having been withdrawn from service in March 1987. This special working was the last train to convey passengers to the town and the only recorded diesel hauled passenger train known to have worked through to Framlingham.
Copyright Malcolm R. White

Another scene at Framlingham but showing a Class 15 Bo-Bo diesel locomotive standing in the platform on a short goods train. Also known as BTH Class 1 locomotives, this type was designed by British Thomson-Houston and built by the Yorkshire Engine Company and the Clayton Equipment Company between 1957 and 1961. The engine was a Paxman 16YHXL unit delivering 800hp. Of the 44 locomotives built, all have been scrapped except D8233 which is privately preserved.
Copyright Colour Rail

With the major increase in container traffic and the need for easy and direct access between Felixstowe Docks, Trimley, and beyond, becoming increasingly important, the original 1877 alignment at Felixstowe was restored in 1970. This left Felixstowe Town station with just a single track in use for the passenger service to Ipswich. The large well planned station is seen here after the redundant track work had been recovered. Forming an Ipswich service, a Cravens built Class 105 diesel multiple unit waits to leave Felixstowe Town from the one platform remaining in use. This location is now a car park and trains use the isolated end of this platform.
Copyright Malcolm R. White

Less than a year before total closure, this scene at Haverhill is of particular interest. A Cambridge - Sudbury service provided by a Derby Lightweight diesel multiple unit, Is seen arriving at the station on a cloudy day in 1966. Some passengers may not appreciate the burning oil drum on the platform, no doubt with today's health and safety culture this would not be allowed. The line through Haverhill closed from Monday 6th March 1967 and the site is now owned by the supermarket giant Tesco.
Copyright Malcolm R. White

Two December 1969 views of the now demolished station at Sudbury. In contrast to the large station seen here, the present one consists of a small platform and a bus-stop type shelter. With the closure of the railway routes north to Cambridge and Bury St. Edmunds via Long Melford, Sudbury once again became a terminus. In the background of the top photograph, recovered track can just be made out in the falling snow to the left of the two car Gloucester Railway Carriage and Wagon Company diesel multiple unit.
Both above photographs copyright Malcolm R. White

The scene looking in the Yarmouth direction through the glass partition in the end compartment of a Metropolitan-Cammell Class 101 diesel multiple unit leaving Corton station. The remaining single track and the disused station building can be seen in this view which was recorded on the last day of passenger services between Yarmouth South Town and Lowestoft Central.
Copyright Malcolm R. White

Top Left - Class 31/1 A1A-A1A No. 31108 passes Ipswich Goods Junction signal box with a south bound express in 1981. Originally No. D5526, and at one time allocated to Ipswich (32B), this Type 2 was withdrawn from service in 1991 and purchased for preservation in 1995. *Copyright Malcolm R. White* **Top Right** - Stratford's Class 47/4 Co-Co No. 47583 *County of Hertfordshire* waits to leave Ipswich with a London train. This Type 4 was initially No. D1767 and in addition to No. 47583, was also 47172 and finally 47734. As 47734, it was scrapped in 2008. *Copyright Norman Fairhead* **Bottom Right** - Now modelled by Hornby in 00 gauge and preserved, Regional Railways No. 37414 *Cathays C & W Works 1846-1993* is seen at Ipswich in 1993. Originally Class 37/0 Co-Co No. D6987, this later became No. 37287 and after being fitted with electric train supply and an alternator became Class 37/4 No. 37414. *Copyright Malcolm R. White /C. Riley*

The majority of railway lines in Suffolk do not support electric traction but much freight and passenger traffic is seen at Ipswich using this type of power. Class 86/4 Bo-Bo No. 86417 *The Kingsman* and Class 86/6 Bo-Bo No. 86610 head a container train into the tunnel at Ipswich in October 1990. In the Inter-City livery is No. 86417 which was originally E3146 whilst the leading locomotive, No. 86610, was originally E3104.
Copyright Malcolm R. White / S. Jordan

Dual braked Class 37 Co-Co No. 37106 emerges from Ipswich tunnel with a flask train for Sizewell on Thursday 13th July 1995. This locomotive started life in early 1963 as No. D6806 and was withdrawn in March 1999. In August 2000, No. 37106 was scrapped. It is seen here in "Dutch" livery, so called because it resembles the livery carried by passenger trains in Holland. This livery was carried by locomotives in the UK assigned to Civil Engineering duties. The depot plaque mounted on the locomotive appears to show the Stratford cockney sparrow.
Copyright Norman Fairhead

After many years without a railway, few people would have believed that a main line steam locomotive would ever be seen at Clare again. However, as part of a special event, North Norfolk Railway based Class J15 0-6-0 No. 65462 visited Clare Country Park in May 2004. The former station is now part of the Park, and the J15 was positioned in light steam on a length of track near the Information Centre, which is housed in the former goods shed. Following this appearance, No. 65462 was taken to the GB Railfreight open day at March depot.

Bottom Right - The view from Clare Castle of the J15 and the surrounding area. The former station can be seen in the top left of the photograph. **Top Left** - No. 65462, the former goods shed and part of the castle on the far right. **Top Right** - No. 65462 and an attending fire engine.
All photographs copyright Malcolm R. White

A bygone feature of Ipswich was the comprehensive access that the railway had to the dock and waterfront areas. This enabled vast quantities of goods to be carried by rail to and from the docks. With the regeneration of the dock area and changes in the commercial port of Ipswich, the railway is no longer required and has been erased from the scene. Only Griffin Wharf on the West Bank retains rail facilities and these are in regular use. These two superb images of tanker wagons heading for the Fisons works will bring back happy memories to many local folk. Images of steam locomotives at work around the docks can be found elsewhere in this book.

Top - On Monday 15th August 1983, Class 03 0-6-0 No. 03179 crosses Bridge Street to gain access to the dock area. In late 2009, this crossing remained intact but was isolated with the railway track either side now buried or recovered. Powered by a Gardner 8L3 engine developing 204hp, the locomotive seen here was one of 230 built by British Railways and was originally No. D2179.

Bottom - With the New Cut on the left, the same train heads for the Fisons works. The railway track in this area is now covered over with tarmac or has been recovered.
Both photographs copyright John Chalfont
www.railphotoprints.co.uk

A number of steam hauled railtours have visited or passed through various Suffolk towns in recent years. On Saturday 18th September 2004, Class BB 4-6-2 No 34067 *Tangmere* visited Lowestoft. Arriving from London Liverpool Street via Norwich, the railtour returned to London via the East Suffolk line. *Tangmere* is seen here reversing the train into platform four after being serviced in Lowestoft sidings.
Copyright David J. White

On Saturday 16th May 2009, another railtour visited Lowestoft this time hauled by Class 7MT 4-6-2 No. 70013 *Oliver Cromwell.* The train is seen here crossing the A12 trunk road at Darsham on the East Suffolk line. This railtour followed the same route as that taken by *Tangmere.*
Copyright Malcolm R. White

RAILWAY MARITIME INTERESTS

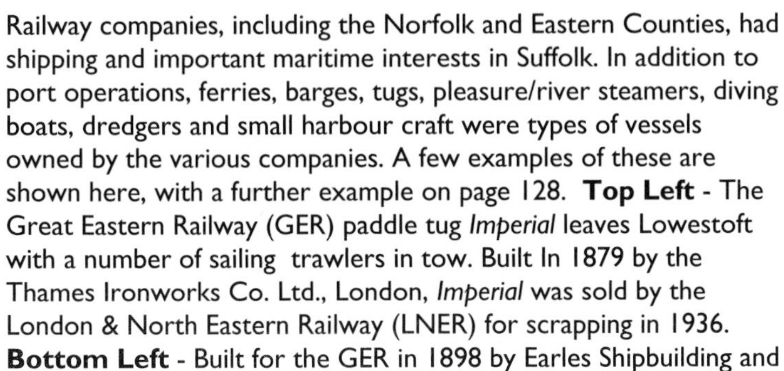

Railway companies, including the Norfolk and Eastern Counties, had shipping and important maritime interests in Suffolk. In addition to port operations, ferries, barges, tugs, pleasure/river steamers, diving boats, dredgers and small harbour craft were types of vessels owned by the various companies. A few examples of these are shown here, with a further example on page 128. **Top Left** - The Great Eastern Railway (GER) paddle tug *Imperial* leaves Lowestoft with a number of sailing trawlers in tow. Built In 1879 by the Thames Ironworks Co. Ltd., London, *Imperial* was sold by the London & North Eastern Railway (LNER) for scrapping in 1936. **Bottom Left** - Built for the GER in 1898 by Earles Shipbuilding and Engineering Co. Ltd., Hull, the screw tug *Lowestoft* was reboilered in 1935 by the LNER, and sold for scrapping at Oulton Broad by British Railways in 1954. **Top Right** - An impressive scene at Ipswich with three railway owned doubled ended pleasure steamers in the New Cut. Nearest is the *Norfolk*, built for the GER in 1900 and sold by the LNER in 1931. **Bottom Right** - Built for the GER in 1896, the *Essex* is also seen here in the New Cut. She was one of two similar vessels, the other being the *Suffolk*. which was built in 1895. The *Essex* was sold by the GER in 1913 and the *Suffolk* by the LNER in 1931.

All photographs from the Malcolm R. White Collection

A FURTHER SELECTION OF SUFFOLK RAILWAY SCENES

A scene familiar to Aldeburgh residents and visitors for almost 100 years, but today the location is difficult to find. This is the approach to the town's station showing the forecourt and car park on the afternoon of Tuesday 23rd April 1963. Compared to the size of the local population when it opened, the station seemed quite large. However, it was expected that the town would grow with a corresponding increase in population and the holiday industry would also develop bringing an increased number of travellers to the town. Aldeburgh was open to passengers from Thursday 12th April 1860 until the crowded last train ran on the evening of Saturday 10th September 1966.
Photographer Andrew Muckley

A comprehensive view of the railway at Aldeburgh on Monday 14th May 1956. This photograph shows the main features of this terminus except the engine shed, which was to the left of the photographer. Locomotive coaling and watering facilities can be seen behind the signal box. The 6.45pm Aldeburgh - Saxmundham train is about to leave hauled by Class J15 0-6-0 No. 65447.
Copyright R.M. Casserley
Photographer H.C. Casserley

A further three scenes recorded at Aldeburgh on Monday 14th May 1956, all featuring Class J15 0-6-0 No. 65447. This was built at Stratford in 1899 as Great Eastern Railway Class Y14 No. 647.

Top Left - The 5.52pm Saxmundham - Aldeburgh train arrives at this terminus station. The building on the left is the goods shed.

Top Right - The 6.45pm Aldeburgh - Saxmundham train is ready to depart.

Bottom Left - No. 65447 prepares to run into the platform to join the carriages forming the 6.45pm train to Saxmundham. These were the same set that had formed the 5.52pm from Saxmundham and the locomotive had just run round the carriages for the journey back to Saxmundham. The engine shed is behind the locomotive.

Photographer H.C. Casserley

Class B12/3 4-6-0 No. 61535 was perhaps the best known of the Ipswich allocated members of this class. In immaculate condition, No. 61535 is seen here at work in the early 1950s on the Aldeburgh - Saxmundham line. After being stored at Stratford for two months, No. 61535 was scrapped there in January 1960.
Courtesy Allan Wood Collection

Aldeburgh station, goods shed, sidings, yard and engine shed covered a large area. In this view, from the signal box at the end of the platform, the goods shed has been demolished, but materials are still being delivered by rail to Aldeburgh. Forming a passenger service to Ipswich, one of the then familiar Metropolitan-Cammell Class 101 diesel multiple units waits to depart.
Copyright Malcolm R. White

Aspall & Thorndon station on the Mid Suffolk Light Railway. The level crossing at the platform end is on the B1077 road.
Courtesy Past Times Prints

The remains of the platform at Aspall & Thorndon in late 2009.
Copyright Malcolm R. White

The interior of the signal box at Barnby.
Copyright Stuart Jones

Barnby signal box with the siding on the left disappearing behind the signal box. This location is known for the serious collision between two trains in 1891. *Copyright Stuart Jones*

Top Left - Barnham was between Seven Hills Halt and Thetford Bridge, and served the villages of Euston, Barnham and Elveden. This early 1950s view of the station is looking north in the Thetford direction.
Copyright HMRS/H. F. Hilton Collection
Top Right - At one time many military camps and airfields existed in Suffolk and this view of a military lorry being used to collect or deliver goods at a station was not uncommon. This 1949 scene shows the siding and signal box at Barnham at a time of heightened tension across Europe.
Copyright HMRS/H. F. Hilton Collection
Bottom Right - Class D16/3 4-4-0 No. 62546 *Claud Hamilton* leads classmate No. 62597 on an up passenger train between Woodbridge and Bealings in 1949. The *Claud Hamilton* nameplates were originally carried by GER Class S46 4-4-0 No. 1900. and were transferred to No. 62546 in 1947.
Copyright E. M. Johnson
Photographer John Hart

Unlike some other closed railway stations, Bealings retains much of the appearance it did when it was open to passengers and served the village of Little Bealings. The station is seen here in the late 1940s with the large goods shed on the left. Goods handled at the station included agricultural produce, coal and items destined for Martlesham Heath airfield. Bealings closed in September 1956 and today almost all the buildings remain. A business centre has been established at the former station using the railway buildings, some of which have been tastefully extended.
Malcolm R. White Collection

This comprehensive view of Beccles was recorded in 1911 when the station was busy with both goods traffic and passenger numbers. In 1953, the station suffered the loss of the passenger service to Tivetshall (for Norwich) followed six years later by the loss of the high profile direct passenger route to Yarmouth. The Midland Railway trucks seen on the left of this photograph near the gate, are standing on the line to the now demolished maltings.
Copyright HMRS/H. F. Hilton Collection

An unusual and interesting scene at Beccles showing LNER E4 2-4-0 No. 2787 taking water in the early evening of Saturday 28th June 1947. As BR No. 62787, this locomotive was condemned in November 1956 and scrapped at Stratford.
Courtesy Past Times Publishing

In pale winter sunshine, T.W. Worsdell designed Class J15 0-6-0 No. 65460 is seen with a pick up goods at Beccles during the afternoon of Saturday 16th February 1957. Completed at Stratford in 1912 as GER Class Y14 0-6-0 No. 562, this locomotive was renumbered 7562 by the LNER in 1924. At the time this scene was recorded, No. 65460 was fitted with a tablet catcher.
Copyright David J. White

On Saturday 1st September 1951, the 9.00am Beccles - Tivetshall train is seen in the bay platform at Beccles waiting to depart on the 19½ mile journey along the Waveney Valley line. There were nine intermediate stations on this line with only Bungay being in Suffolk. Norwich allocated Class E4 2-4-0 No. 62789 is heading the train which was due to arrive at Tivetshall at 9.50am. With the advertised connection there for Norwich, passengers should have been at Thorpe station by 10.16am. The timetable below gives further details of Waveney Valley line services.
Copyright R.M. Casserley
Photographer H.C. Casserley

TIVETSHALL, BUNGAY, and BECCLES

Week Days only

Miles from Tivetshall		a.m		a.m		a.m		a.m		p.m		p.m	
	3 London (L'pool St.) dep	..	..	4 30	..	8 30	..	11 30	..	1 30	..	5 30	..
	3 Norwich (Thorpe) "	6 55	..	7 55	..	10 54	..	12 55	..	5 3	..	7 23	..
	3 Forncett........ "	6 57	..	8 19	..	11 18	..	1 19	..	5 27	..	7 49	..
—	Tivetshall..........dep	7 19	..	8 35	..	11 25	..	2 15	..	5 36	..	8 15	..
2¾	Pulham Market..........	7 25	..	8 41	..	11 31	..	2 21	..	5 42	..	8 21	..
3½	Pulham St. Mary.......	7 28	..	8 44	..	11 34	..	2 24	..	5 45	..	8 24	..
6¼	Harleston...............	7 36	..	8 56	..	11 41	..	2 32	..	5 51	..	8 36	..
9	Homersfield	7 42	..	9 2	..	11 47	..	2 38	..	5 57	..	8 42	..
12	Earsham	7 48	..	9 8	..	11 53	..	2 44	..	6 3	..	8 48	..
13	Bungay	7 52	..	9D20	..	11 56	..	2 47	..	6 7	..	8 51	..
13¾	Ditchingham	7 57	..	9 24	..	12 0	..	2 51	..	6 11	..	8 55	..
15¼	Ellingham	8 1	..	9 28	..	12 4	..	2 55	..	6 15	..	8 59	..
17¾	Geldeston	8 5	..	9 32	..	12 8	..	2 59	..	6 19	..	9 3	..
19½	Beccles............... arr	8 11	..	9 38	..	12 14	..	3 5	..	6 25	..	9 9	..
28	3 Lowestoft (C.) .. arr	8 53	..	1010	..	12 59	..	3 42	..	7 16	..	9 46	..
32	3 Yarmouth (S.T.). "	8 45	..	1012	..	1 12	..	4Z45	..	7 20	..	9 45	..
128½	3 London (L'pool St.) "	11U34	..	1B30	..	3‡56	..	6 48	..	9 46	..	..	..

Week Days only

Miles from Beccles		a.m		a.m		a.m		p.m		p.m		p.m	
	3 London (L'pool St. dep	..	..	4 30	..	9S33	..	12S33	..	3 33	..	4 30	..
	3 Yarmouth (S.T.). "	6 35	..	8 20	..	12 10	..	2 55	..	6 20	..	7 20	..
	3 Lowestoft (C.)... "	6 36	..	8 20	..	12K10	..	2 55	..	6 20	..	7 31	..
—	Beccles.............dep	7 0	..	9 0	..	12 35	..	3 25	..	6 55	..	8 2	..
2¼	Geldeston	7 6	..	9 6	..	12 41	..	3 31	..	7 1	..	8 8	..
4¼	Ellingham	7 10	..	9 10	..	12 45	..	3 35	..	7 5	..	8 12	..
5¾	Ditchingham............	7 14	..	9 14	..	12 49	..	3 39	..	7 9	..	8 16	..
6½	Bungay	7 19	..	9 19	..	12 53	..	3 44	..	7 13	..	8 20	..
7¼	Earsham	7 22	..	9 22	..	12 56	..	3 47	..	7 16	..	8 23	..
10½	Homersfield	7 29	..	9 29	..	1 3	..	3 54	..	7 23	..	8 30	..
13¼	Harleston................	7 35	..	9 35	..	1 9	..	4 1	..	7 30	..	8 40	..
15¾	Pulham St. Mary	7 41	..	9 41	..	1 15	..	4 7	..	7 36	..	8 46	..
16¾	Pulham Market..........	7 44	..	9 44	..	1 18	..	4 10	..	7 39	..	8 49	..
19½	Tivetshall............arr	7 50	..	9 50	..	1 24	..	4 18	..	7 45	..	8 55	..
22	3 Forncett........arr	8 5	..	9 59	..	1 41	..	4 30	..	..	..	9 7	..
24	3 Norwich (Thorpe) "	8 30	..	1016	..	2 4	..	4 53	..	8 29	..	9 30	..
120	3 London (L'pool St.) "	11 18	..	1L30	..	4H34	..	7 45	..	12a7	..	2A33	..

NOTES

A a.m. Via Norwich (Thorpe) and Ely
a a.m.
B Arr. 1 16 p.m. on Mons., Fris. and Sats.
D Arr. 9 10 a.m.
H Arr. 4 20 p.m. on Fridays and 4 16 p.m. on Saturdays
K Dep. 12 5 p.m. on Saturdays
L Arr. 1 20 p.m. on Saturdays
S Saturdays only
U From 25th July to 6th September arr. 11 30 a.m. on Fridays and 11 27 a.m. on Saturdays
Z Arr. 3 41 p.m. on Saturdays
‡ Arr. 3 11 p.m. on Saturdays

The summer 1952 timetable for trains between Beccles, Bungay, Harleston and Tivetshall. This once important service provided a transport link across a large rural area and at Beccles and Tivetshall enabled connections to be made to two important main lines that gave access to large towns, cities and coastal resorts.
Malcolm R. White Collection

Bentley station was on the London to Norwich main line between Ipswich and Manningtree and is where the branch line from Hadleigh terminated. This 1955 view is from the level crossing at the station and looking in the Ipswich direction, with the down and bay platforms on the left. Until February 1932, when the service was withdrawn, passengers using Hadleigh services transferred to and from main line services here.
Copyright Stations UK

The last passenger train from Bentley to Hadleigh ran on Saturday 27th February 1932. A few minutes prior to departure, the station master and some of the station staff gathered on the platform next to the locomotive hauling the train, for a commemorative photograph with the driver and fireman.
Courtesy Past Times Publishing

Stratford allocated Class 7MT 4-6-2 No. 70000 *Britannia* approaches Bentley with an up express on Saturday 9th June 1956. Designed at Derby and introduced in 1951, fifty five of this class were built and *Britannia* is one of two examples still in existence. The Bentley - Hadleigh branch, goods only since 1932, is on the left. *Copyright HMRS/J. J .Davis Collection*

Blythburgh station on the narrow gauge Southwold Railway was situated between Walberswick and Wenhaston stations. Opening in September 1879, the railway closed in April 1929. The bridge seen here carried the A12 trunk road over the railway and this was demolished in 1962. *Malcolm Maclean Collection*

The railway between Ipswich and Bury St. Edmunds opened in late 1846 and the timber built station at Bramford opened at the same time. The station was located close to a bridge carrying the railway over the B1067 road. Following a fire in 1912, it was rebuilt in brick but on the other side of the bridge from the original. The later Bramford station, which is seen here in the process of being painted, closed in May1955.
Courtesy Past Times Publishing

Today Brampton station consists of a single track platform and a bus stop type shelter. All the buildings and the signal box seen here in the 1960s, have been demolished. Out of view on the now demolished down platform was a shelter that at one time was at Great Ormesby station and can now be found at Mangapps Farm Railway Museum.
Copyright Stuart Jones

Brandon station is between Thetford and Lakenheath on the Norwich - Ely line and this view of the station in 1911 is looking in the Ely direction. The main goods yard is on the right and the station is in the top middle of the photograph. In the bottom right corner two horses engaged in shunting can just be seen.
Courtesy Past Times Publishing

Brandon has staggered platforms and these are demonstrated in this pre-grouping photograph. This view is looking in the Norwich direction with the main station building on the left. The bridge seen here has been replaced by a different one, positioned in almost the same location. Sidings, additional to those seen here, were on the down or Norwich side of the station and these are seen in the previous photograph. The now demolished water tower, toilets and waiting shelter were on the up platform on the right.
Courtesy Past Times Prints

Today Brockford is the location of the Mid Suffolk Light Railway Museum which includes a very realistic recreation of a Mid Suffolk Light Railway station. This pleasant scene recorded there in 1952, shows Class J15 0-6-0 No. 65459 at Brockford with a Haughley bound train. Brockford station was close to the village of Wetheringsett.
Courtesy Mid Suffolk Light Railway Museum

On Sunday 14th July 2002 a different Class J15 locomotive was at Brockford when No. 65462, normally to be found on the North Norfolk Railway, paid a visit. Suitably polished and with GER on the tender, the J15 arrives at the recreated station with a train of two fully restored coaches. The second of these, GER Officers Saloon No. 14, was on loan from Stately Trains. This was completed in December 1889 at Stratford Works and when no longer required for passenger carrying duties, spent many years in departmental service at Ipswich.
Copyright Malcolm R. White

An uncommon view of Bungay station forecourt with horse drawn carriages and two Great Eastern Railway motor omnibuses in attendance. The 1860 built wooden station building was replaced in 1933 with one of brick construction. It is believed this print originates from 1912 when train services between Bungay and Harleston were suspended due to flooding, and the railway company brought in omnibuses to maintain services where the line was damaged.
Courtesy Past Times Publishing

Bungay station and yard covered a large area and was one of the places where trains could pass on the line between Beccles and Tivetshall. Lowestoft allocated Class F4 2-4-2T No. 67167 pauses at the station whilst working a Tivetshall to Beccles train on a sunny Tuesday 22nd July 1952. This scene was recorded from under the arches of the now demolished bridge at the station.
Copyright Mid Railway Trust, Ripley

Top Left and Right - Class J15 0-6-0 No. 65447 of Ipswich shed with the Railway Enthusiasts Club railtour of Sunday 30th September 1956 at Bungay. Despite not offering a passenger service since 1953, the station appears very well maintained and tidy.
Both photographs copyright R. M. Casserley

Bottom Right - A busy time at Bungay with the token being handed over from an unidentified Class J15 0-6-0 heading a Beccles bound train as it passes an unidentified Class E4 2-4-0 heading a Tivetshall bound train. Fortunately examples of both types of locomotive still exists in 2010. A Class J15 0-6-0 is maintained in working order at the North Norfolk Railway, and a Class E4 2-4-0 can be found at the steam museum at Bressingham as a static exhibit.
Courtesy Anglian Rail Archive

Above - A comprehensive view showing Bungay yard, signal box and goods shed in 1947. All evidence of the railway at this location has been swept away for new road construction. This view is looking east from the now demolished bridge at the station that allowed vehicles to gain access to Bungay Common.
Courtesy Anglian Rail Archive

Left - Two views of Class F4 2-4-2T No. 67158 on Monday 21st July 1952 at Bungay whilst working a Beccles - Tivetshall train. In the top photograph, the W. H. Smith bookstall can be seen on the right, and in the bottom photograph the bridge mentioned in previous captions, and the goods shed can be seen. The exit to the town from the station is on the right.
Both photographs copyright Mid Railway Trust, Ripley

Gardner powered Class 03 0-6-0 diesel shunter No. D2034 (later renumbered 03034) stands at Bungay with the goods train from Beccles and Lowestoft, only a few months before closure of this goods only terminus. Until January 1953, when passenger services were withdrawn, Bungay had been a busy two platform intermediate station on the Waveney Valley line between Beccles and Tivetshall in Norfolk. The station was recorded here in March 1964, with some track already recovered, buildings demolished and awaiting final closure. Only isolated parts of the Waveney Valley line were in Suffolk, and these included Beccles and Bungay stations. The railway has been totally erased from the landscape at this location which is now part of the busy A143 road.

Copyright Malcolm R. White
Photographer Dr. Ian C. Allen

On Friday 20th April 1951, a Colchester - Cambridge passenger train headed by Class E4 2-4-0 No. 62794 makes for Bures after leaving Chappel. The journey via the Stour Valley line took some steam hauled services over two hours and involved stopping at fifteen stations including Sudbury, Haverhill and Long Melford.
Malcolm R. White Collection

Bures was one of only two Suffolk stations to survive following the closure of the majority of the Stour Valley line in 1967. This 1962 view is looking in the Marks Tey direction and shows the now demolished station building and signal box. A long standing shed type structure now provides shelter for passengers. Bures is situated between Chappel and Wakes Colne station and the branch line terminus at Sudbury. In 2010, the service is mainly hourly and usually provided by Class 153 or 156 diesel multiple units
Copyright Stations UK

Of the two buildings seen here in this pre-grouping view, the building on the left is the now demolished Bures station. The shed mentioned in the previous caption is to the left of the main building.
Copyright Lens of Sutton Association

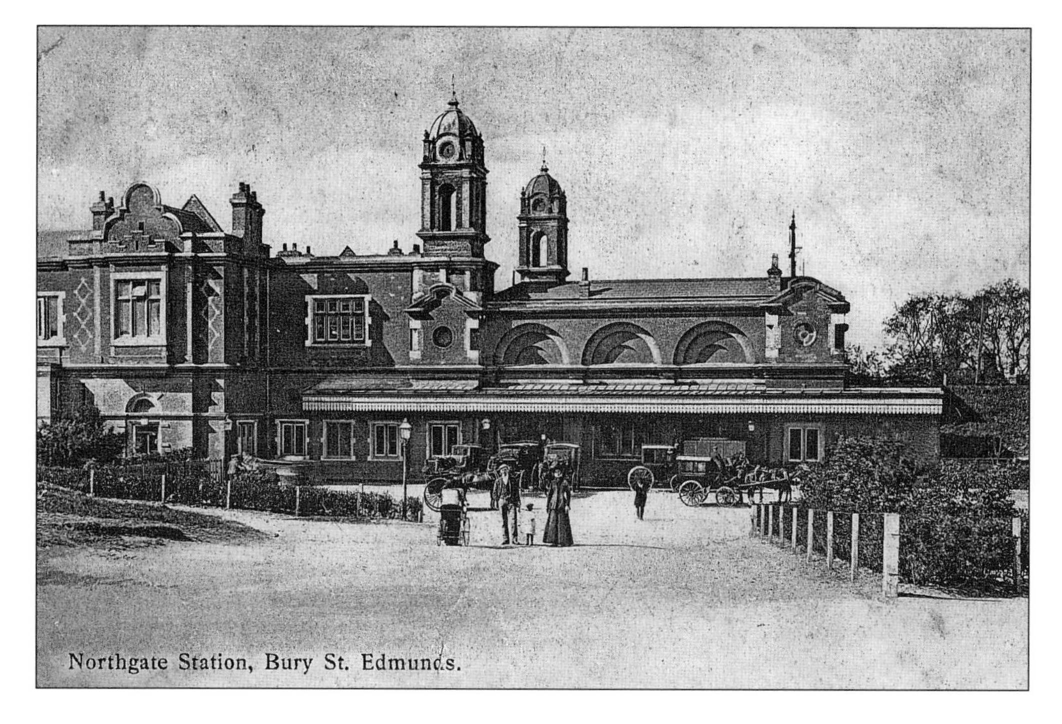

A fine view of Bury St. Edmunds Northgate station on sale as a postcard in 1910. The building is basically the same today, although the canopy over the entrance has been reduced in length. A noteworthy aspect of the east end of the building are the two towers, one on each of the two platforms. Constructed of red brick with stone dressings, the station was built as a terminus with a train shed roof, four tracks and one platform. West of the building, a turntable and engine shed were located. These were removed to allow construction of the railway to Newmarket in 1854. This station became known as Bury St. Edmunds following the the closure of the other station in the town at Eastgate Street.
Malcolm R. White Collection

On Sunday 6th September 1953, the London Branch of the Railway Correspondence and Travel Society organised an East Anglian Railtour that started from Bishopsgate Goods Depot and after visiting MarksTey, Bury St. Edmunds, Cambridge and Hitchin, ended at London Liverpool Street. Three different locomotives were used on the tour including Bishop Stortford allocated Class J20/1 0-6-0 No. 64685 which is seen here at Bury St. Edmunds.
The Class J20s were designed by A.J. Hill and introduced in 1920. Many were rebuilt in 1943 with a different boiler creating the Class J20/1.
Photographer A. W. Burges
Copyright Andrew Ingram

A 1950s view of Bury St. Edmunds looking east from the down platform showing the station's twin towers and Parkeston allocated Gresley Class K3/2 2-6-0 No. 61942 taking water whilst working a cross country service. The two through lines were recovered when the track layout and signalling were modernised.
Copyright Essex Bus Enthusiasts Group
Photographer Frank Church

Top Left - Looking west from the up platform at Bury St. Edmunds as Ipswich allocated Class B12/3 4-6-0 No. 61564 passes through the station. The locomotive depot (31E) can be seen in the distance. This Gresley rebuild of a Holden GER design was scrapped at Stratford Works in December 1958. One of these fine locomotives, No. 61572, is preserved today on the North Norfolk Railway.
Copyright Essex Bus Enthusiasts Group
Photographer Frank Church

Top Right - An atmospheric view of the three road Bury St. Edmunds engine shed with Cambridge allocated Class J17 0-6-0 No. 65562 one of two locomotives on shed. Opening in 1904, this was the third engine shed to be built at Bury St. Edmunds and was provided by the GER. The first was constructed to coincide with the opening of the line to Ipswich in 1846, and the second was built to replace the first, which was removed around 1854 in connection with the building of the line to Newmarket.
Courtesy Allan Wood Collection

Bottom Right - Opened in 1865, Bury St. Edmunds Eastgate was a small intermediate station on the Bury St. Edmunds - Long Melford line. This closed in 1909 and nothing remains of the station.
Malcolm R. White Collection

A Cravens Class 105 diesel multiple unit waits to depart from the down platform at Bury St. Edmunds for Colchester, via Long Melford, on Saturday 25th March 1961. The passenger service on the Bury St. Edmunds - Long Melford line was withdrawn the following month, after which the distance to Colchester by rail was considerably longer with an extended journey time. One of the two towers at the east end of the station and the four tracks through the station can be seen.
Courtesy Past Times Prints

Capel station was close to the village of Capel St. Mary and one of the stations on the Bentley - Hadleigh branch line. The station was designed by Frederick Barnes and unfinished when it opened to goods services in August 1847 and to passengers the following month. It closed in February 1932 to passengers and to goods traffic in April 1965. Capel was adjacent to the A12 trunk road which can be seen in this view of the station. The road crossing was equipped with warning lights and additional warning signs as well as the manually operated level crossing gates. Today the A12 is an extremely busy dual carriageway road at this point, in contrast to that seen here.
Malcolm R. White Collection

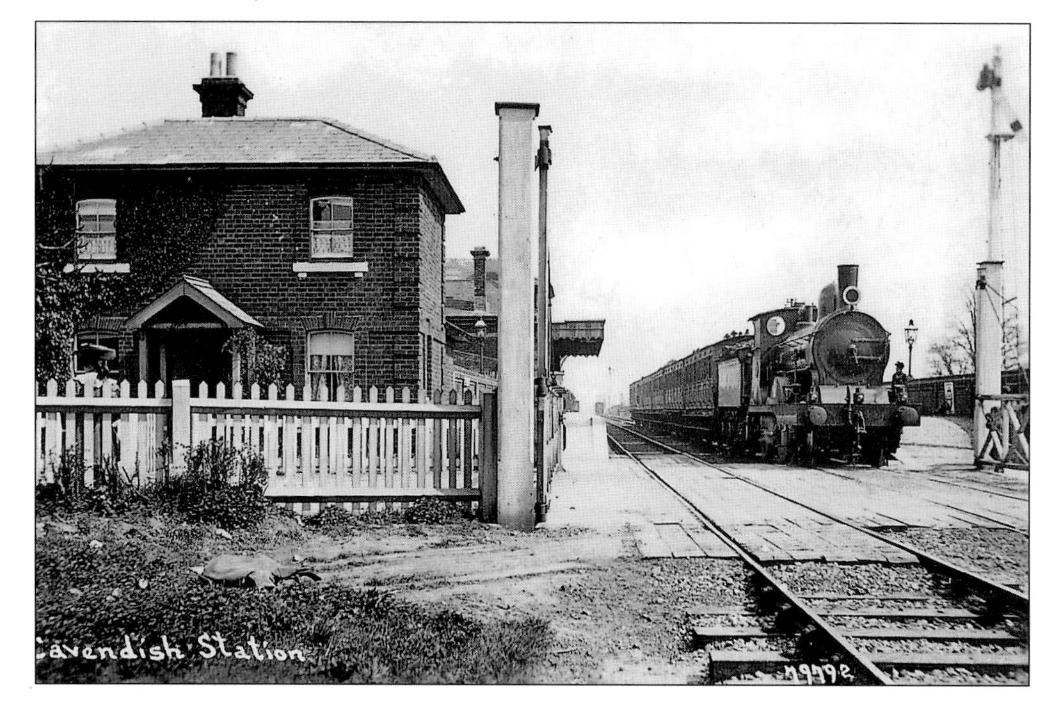

Cavendish station looking east towards Long Melford with GER Class T26 2-4-0 No. 426 at the station with a west-bound passenger train. The gatekeepers house on the left exists today as a private residence and a small section of platform remains adjacent to the house. However much of the land behind this property together with the station site has been developed for housing. Completed at Stratford in 1891, No. 426 was condemned in October 1926 as LNER Class E4 2-4-0 No. 7426.
Courtesy Foxearth and District Local History Society

The following five photographs originated from Mr. Bernard Saunders, the last signal man at Cavendish. They show different aspects of this former GER station.

Into the British Railway era and Class E4 2-4-0 No. 62790 brings a Cambridge - Colchester train over the level crossing and into the platform. The single line to Clare can be seen on the other side of the crossing. Completed in September 1896, No. 62790 was condemned in January 1956.
Copyright Foxearth and District Local History Society

Looking west towards Clare from Cavendish and showing the level crossing, well maintained platforms and fine shrubs.

A view from a train arriving at Cavendish in the 1950s.

The signal box, platforms and the well maintained shrubs at Cavendish looking east towards Glemsford. Nothing remains of this scene today.

The last day of services at Cavendish and a diesel multiple unit, the leading carriage of which is Cravens Railway Carriage & Wagon Co. Class 141 driving trailer No. E56437, enters the station.

The former Clare station is now part of a country park with the great majority of the original buildings intact and well maintained. The goods shed, which is behind the photographer, contains an information centre and a restored box van. Looking east towards Cavendish, the main station building is seen here in the late 1950s. An overall view of this location can be found in the colour section.
Courtesy Past Times Publishing

A fine view of the eastern approach to Clare station from Cavendish showing the pleasant wooded environment the former station is set in. The railway station and goods shed were in the inner bailey of the 13th century stone castle which is set upon a 70ft high motte. Those responsible for setting up and maintaining Clare Castle Country Park have admirably preserved the fine collection of former railway buildings and the platforms on this site. Appropriate uses have been found for all the buildings.
Malcolm R. White Collection

Claydon station was designed by Frederick Barnes and like others from his drawing board had a particular charm and style with their Dutch gables and high chimneys. Claydon opened in 1846 and closed in 1963.
Copyright Tom Martin

The view looking towards Lowestoft from Corton station in the early 1960s when a full passenger and goods service was still offered at the station. For many years on Saturdays in the summer, hundreds of holidaymakers would arrive at or depart from the station with many using trains such as the "Holiday Camps Express". Corton opened with the Lowestoft Central - Yarmouth railway line in July 1903, and closed with the line, in May 1970. The main station building on the left exists today as a private residence.
Copyright Stuart Jones

Seen here in GER days, Cockfield was between Welnetham and Lavenham on the Bury St. Edmunds - Long Melford railway line. *Copyright Lens of Sutton Collection*

The platform and station building at Cockfield in 2009. The station closed completely in April 1965. *Copyright Malcolm R. White*

Situated next to the busy A12 trunk road, Darsham has changed little externally from when it was a staffed railway station. At the time of writing, the former station building is in use by the registered charity "The Woodcraft Folk" and known as the "Darsham Country Centre". Sleeping 22 people, the facilities include a spacious kitchen (with disabled access), a dining room, games/recreation room with an open fire, and seven bedrooms. Some visitors to the centre travel by train especially from London on the through services that National Express East Anglia intends withdrawing in 2010. The station, signal box and A12 level crossing are seen here in GER days with a train in the up platform. *Malcolm R. White Collection*

On Sunday 30th September 1956, the 2.52pm Yarmouth South Town - London Liverpool Street train is seen leaving Darsham for London hauled by two of Yarmouth South Town's Class B17 4-6-0 locomotives. Leading is No. 61670 *City of London* followed by *No.* 61665 *Leicester City*. *City of London* was scrapped in April 1960 and *Leicester City* in June 1959. *City of London* was one of the class that were streamlined from 1937 until 1951.
Copyright R.M. Casserley

With the Port of Felixstowe intending to significantly increase the number of containers and other goods carried by rail, a substantial increase in the number of trains passing through Derby Road station in Ipswich is expected. The station is seen here on Monday 14th May 1956 with a passenger train about to leave for Felixstowe.
Copyright R.M. Casserley
Photographer H.C. Casserley

Elmswell 1910-The station, level crossing and signal box. The last stationmaster, from 1959 until 1967, was Mr. Frank Thompson. *Malcolm R. White Collection*

Elmswell 1950-The station building on the down platform. Designed by Mr. Frederick Barnes, this was demolished in 1974 and replaced by a bus-stop type shelter. *Copyright HMRS/H. F. Hilton Collection*

Elmswell 1952-Looking in the Stowmarket direction with the down platform on the left. The building on the up platform still exists and is in use by a travel agent. *Copyright HMRS/H. F. Hilton Collection*

Elmswell 1990s-A more recent view from the level crossing and looking in the Bury St. Edmunds direction, with the down platform in the foreground. *Copyright Malcolm R. White*

At the end of the 3 mile branch line from Mellis, Eye was a compact terminus with an engine shed for the small locomotive used on the line, and a reasonable size goods shed and yard. Opened in April 1867, the branch was considered to be one of the shortest rural railways in the country. The Great Eastern Railway took over the line in 1898 having worked it from the outset. Bricks, coal and a wide range of agricultural products kept the goods traffic at a satisfactory level for many years after the passenger service was withdrawn in February 1931. However, in July 1964 the goods service was withdrawn and the line closed. Looking somewhat like a railroad station in the wild west, this view of Eye dates from 1910.
Copyright HMRS/H. F. Hilton Collection

Eye station in the early 1900s with GER Class E22 0-6-0T No. 249 having just arrived with a passenger train from Mellis. Before the opening of Yaxley Halt, the time for the journey from Mellis was twelve minutes. Built in 1893, No. 249 was scrapped in 1937 as LNER Class J65 No. 7249.
Malcolm R. White Collection

Felixstowe Railway & Pier Co. (FR& PC) No. 2 *Orwell* was one of three similar locomotives supplied by the Yorkshire Engine Co. for use on the new railway to Felixstowe. *Malcolm R. White Collection*

Another of the FR&PC locomotives, No. 3 *Felixstowe,* is seen here as No. 0810 after the GER takeover of the FR&PC. The third locomotive was No. 1 *Tomline. Copyright LCGB/Ken Nunn Collection*

An unusual view of Felixstowe in the early 1900s showing from left to right a small hut with a large notice proclaiming "Felixstowe Dock", the dock offices, Pier Hotel, the large maltings, the railway passenger pier on which the photographer is standing, and the railway booking office. Later a flour mill and several sidings were constructed on the north side of the dock. After the GER began to work the railway from Westerfield to Felixstowe Pier in 1879, the FR&PC retained possession of the dock and the network of associated railways. Colonel George Tomline, a major landowner on the Felixstowe peninsula and the driving force behind the FR&PC, cut the first sod to start work on the dock in 1881.
Malcolm R. White Collection

Felixstowe Pier was one of the original stations opened by the FR&PC in 1877. In peace time it was never regarded as a busy station, however in both World Wars, due to the military presence in the area around the station, it was of great importance both for passenger and goods traffic. The station was closed completely in July 1951, but the railway line leading to the station and original dock basin was later extended into the Felixstowe Dock & Railway Company South container terminal, and has become a busy and vital link to the national network. Pier station is seen here in this 1930s postcard.
Malcolm R. White Collection

No longer in existence, Felixstowe Beach was always popular in the summer months with day trippers and holidaymakers. At one time it was considered the main station for the town and indeed was referred to as Town station. Felixstowe Beach is seen here on Monday 14th May 1956.
Copyright R.M. Casserley
Photographer H.C. Casserley

An unusual view from track level of Felixstowe Beach. Despite many protests, in April 2004 these original FR&PC buildings were demolished. Now frequent container trains pass the overgrown platform and site of the demolished station. This scene was recorded after the station buildings had ceased to be used for passenger services.
Copyright Malcolm R. White

This scene was recorded at Felixstowe Beach on Monday 14th May 1956 looking south towards the closed Felixstowe Pier station and the docks, an area that has seen tremendous development since the 1950s. Whilst the overgrown Beach station platform still exists, the track work seen here has been greatly simplified to just provide access to the South container terminal. As with the station building, the signal box on the left has been demolished.
Copyright R.M. Casserley
Photographer H.C. Casserley

On the same day, Class L1 2-6-4T No. 67739 waits to leave Felixstowe Beach with the 12.45pm to Ipswich. Designed by Edward Thompson and introduced in 1945, these powerful locomotives worked most passenger services between Ipswich and Felixstowe in the early and mid 1950s. Stabled in the bay platform is a set of passenger coaches typical of the type used on services between Felixstowe and Ipswich at that time.
Copyright R.M. Casserley
Photographer H.C. Casserley

It is a sunny day in August 1958 and at Felixstowe Beach passengers alight from a newly arrived train from Ipswich and will no doubt be heading for the seafront, beach or amusement park. Their train, which would have reversed at Town station, is headed by Class L1 2-6-4T No. 67705. Two other Class L1s are present, No. 67715 is at the buffers and another example of the same class is behind that. Both identifiable locomotives were allocated to Ipswich.
The author travelled to Beach station on many occasions in the 1950s and can verify that this was a typical high summer scene, with the station very busy as trains arrived carrying vast numbers of day trippers to the resort.
Malcolm R. White Collection

Closed to passengers in 1967, Felixstowe Beach was one of the original stations on the line from Westerfield, but now only the overgrown platform exists to remind us of this once important station. In the early 1970s, Class 31/1 A1A-A1A No. 5875 (later renumbered 31322) is seen at the disused station as Class 37/0 Co-Co No. 6752 (later renumbered 37052) passes through to the South Terminal with a container train. Felixstowe Beach signal box can be seen at the end of the platform, and departmental stock occupies the bay.

Copyright Malcolm R. White
Photographer Dr. Ian C. Allen

An early morning scene in the 1960s looking towards the docks from Beach Station Road level crossing as 1750bhp Class 37/0 Co-Co No. 6967 approaches with a train from the South container terminal. The Canadian built General Motors 3200bhp Class 66 locomotives have now generally replaced British built machines on this work. This locomotive was renumbered 37267 in 1974 and renumbered again in 1985 as 37421. It is now preserved in Wales at the Pontypool and Blaenavon Railway.
Copyright Malcolm R. White
Photographer Dr. Ian C. Allen

Felixstowe Town was an impressive and well laid out station, most of which is no longer in railway ownership.
The entrance to the station is seen here on Monday 14th May 1956. The majority of this building still exists as a shopping centre containing retail shops and food establishments.
Copyright R.M. Casserley
Photographer H.C.Casserley

In the 1930s, LNER apple green livery Class B12/3 4-6-0 No. 8571 is seen about to be turned on the Felixstowe Town turntable. This was close to Garrison Lane bridge which is immediately to the left in this view. As mentioned elsewhere, the sheds were at Beach station, but a pit and water column could be found at Town station in the late 1930s. This locomotive was allocated to Norwich between October 1957 and December 1959 and was scrapped at Stratford in early 1960. It was one of the last two of the class to be broken up, the other being No. 61535. It is planned to apply the attractive apple green livery to the last remaining Class B12/3 locomotive on the North Norfolk Railway in 2010.
Copyright Jeremy Suter Collection

It is August 1958 and a typical high summer scene at Felixstowe Town as two trains, both headed by Ipswich Class L1 2-6-4T locomotives wait for passengers. On the left is No 67719 on a local working to Ipswich and on the right is No. 67717 with a excursion returning to London Liverpool Street. This locomotive would be exchanged at Ipswich for another, which would take the train through to London.
Courtesy Allan Wood Collection

Originally Felixstowe Town was a well planned substantial station able to cope with the longest trains. Unfortunately, due to railway land and property being sold off in the mid 1980s, the existing much reduced station is never likely to regain the flexibility and capacity the original station had. Once a common sight at the seaside town, an excursion train, in this case hauled by Stratford allocated green liveried English Electric Type 3 Co-Co No. D6711, waits for the day trippers to return to the train for the journey home on Easter Monday 1962. Powered by an English Electric 12cyl. 12CSVT 1750hp engine, D6711 later became Class 37/0 No. 37011 and was scrapped in August 1989.
Courtesy Allan Wood Collection

The present Felixstowe station is part of one of the original platforms. Seen here in the centre of this photograph, the unstaffed isolated terminus seems lost in a sea of cars in this view from the shopping centre known as Great Eastern Square. This was originally the main part of the Great Eastern Railway station.
Copyright Malcolm R. White

Due to rapidly increasing demand for transportation by rail of high volumes of containers and other goods from the Suffolk port in the 1960s, scenes such as this at Felixstowe Town became an everyday occurrence until the 1877 line to the docks was reinstated in April 1970. Class 31/1 A1A-A1A No. D5567 (later renumbered 31149), a Class 37/0 and a Class 105 diesel multiple unit are seen together at the station in the late 1960s. Another view taken from almost the same location is in the colour section of this book and shows the same area a few years later with much of the trackbed seen here rapidly being reclaimed by nature. This is now part of the car park for the adjacent shopping centre.

Photographer Dr. Ian C. Allen

Top Left - A view looking south from the bridge carrying the B1113 road over the railway at Finningham. This scene is in GER days and shows a permanent way train in the platform. Midland Railway wagons can be seen on the left. *Copyright Lens of Sutton Association* **Top Right** - A number of changes had taken place by the time this scene was recorded from the same bridge on Friday 12th June 1953. These include the demolition of the gents toilets and alterations to the shelter on the down platform. *Courtesy James Marshall* **Bottom Left** - Finningham was one of a number of Suffolk stations on the main line between Ipswich and Norwich that closed in the 1950s and 60s. This station opened to goods in June 1848, and to passengers in July 1849 with the opening of the Haughley to Burston section of track. Finningham closed in November 1966 and this early 1960s view is looking north towards Mellis, another closed Suffolk station.
Courtesy Past Times Prints

Externally, Framlingham station changed little when the passenger services were withdrawn but the goods service was retained. The station is seen here in 1960.
Copyright Stuart Jones

The railway to Framlingham is one of several in Suffolk no longer in existence. Ipswich allocated Class F6 2-4-2 No. 67230 was a regular performer on this and the Aldeburgh branch and is seen here about to leave Framlingham with an afternoon train to Wickham Market. Much of the trackbed to Framlingham has been erased from the landscape and the railway line is now difficult to trace in many places.
Courtesy Allan Wood Collection

This unusual view of Framlingham shows the platform occupied by a recently arrived passenger train headed by Class J15 0-6-0 No. 65467 of Ipswich shed. This scene was recorded on Monday 5th December 1949.
Copyright Andrew C. Ingram

Many years after the last passenger train had left Framlingham, Class 31/1 A1A-A1A No. D5520 (later renumbered 31102) leaves the town's station with a short goods train.
Copyright Malcolm R. White
Photographer Dr. Ian C. Allen

This view of Glemsford station was used on an early postcard and is seen from what is now the A1092 road. The level crossing is next to the railway house on the left.

Glemsford station as seen from the level crossing. The railway house, which still exists as a private dwelling, is to the right of this photograph. Tickets were purchased on the train in the final year.

The final passenger train leaves Glemsford for Cavendish on Saturday 4th March 1967, the last day of passenger services. The line closed from Monday 6th March 1967 but there was no Sunday passenger service on this part of the Stour Valley line. The train is formed by a Derby Lightweight diesel multiple unit. These units soon became a familiar sight throughout the county after being introduced in 1954.

A photograph believed taken in 1906 at Hadleigh, showing a passenger train having just arrived from Bentley hauled by a Holden designed tank locomotive. *Malcolm R. White Collection*

This view shows Hadleigh station in the early 1950s when the branch from Bentley was used for goods traffic only. The main entrance to the building is on the left. *Malcolm R. White Collection*

With the station still unfinished, the first goods services to Hadleigh were in August 1847, with passenger services commencing the following month. At one time it was hoped that the railway would be extended through to Lavenham and then to the Midlands. Passenger services were withdrawn in February 1932 but goods services continued until April 1965. Dominated by the maltings, this is Hadleigh in 1925 with a good selection of wagons representing several railway companies in the sidings. *Copyright Stations UK*

The view from the station footbridge at Halesworth showing a London bound express approaching the up platform where many passengers are waiting. On the right is the large dairy, for many years a well known feature of the station. The level crossing for the A144 Norwich Road can be clearly seen. This was in use until the late 1950s when a new road bridge was constructed rendering the level crossing redundant. The crossing gates/platform sections, refurbished in 1999, are now permanently fixed.
Copyright Lens of Sutton Association

Later demolished and replaced by a bus-stop type shelter, the station building on the up platform is quite prominent in this view of Halesworth. Beyond the platform can be seen the signal box that is now at County School station on the Mid Norfolk Railway. The one time movable platform sections, mentioned in the previous caption and elsewhere in this book, can be identified on both platforms where the wood surface replaces the tarmac.
Copyright Malcolm R. White

An unusual view of Halesworth with Class 31/1 A1A-A1A locomotive No. D5575 (later renumbered 31157) in the sidings behind the up platform. On the far right and not visible in this view is the large dairy where milk tankers can be seen at the loading platform. The land in the foreground and where the sidings are is now a road and the site of the dairy is now occupied by housing.

Copyright Malcolm R. White.
Photographer Dr. Ian C. Allen

Sharp, Stewart 2-4-2T No. 1 *Southwold* waits at Halesworth station to depart with a Southwold train. Built in 1893, this locomotive was the second to have this identity. *Courtesy Malcolm Maclean Collection*

Built in 1879 by Sharp, Stewart and possibly in the early green livery, 2-4-0T No. 2 *Halesworth* is seen at Halesworth with the dome and brasswork well polished. *Courtesy Malcolm Maclean Collection*

The same area at Halesworth seen in the photograph on page 95 but much earlier, with the Southwold Railway track on the right, standard gauge track and stock in the centre, and between them the transhipment platform. On the far left is the Great Eastern Railway (GER) main line from Ipswich to Lowestoft and Great Yarmouth. The footbridge seen here gave access from the GER up and down platforms to the Southwold Railway island platforms which are on the right. The bridge carrying the A144 Norwich Road over the railway did not exist at this time, with the road crossing the railway by the level crossing formed by the moveable platforms mentioned elsewhere.
Courtesy Malcolm Maclean Collection

A fine view of the substantial Haughley station building and some of the staff in 1906. Now mainly demolished, Haughley opened in July 1849 and closed to passengers in January 1967.
Malcolm R. White Collection

At the Mid Suffolk Light Railway (MSLR) Haughley station on the afternoon of Thursday 5th August 1909, MSLR 0-6-0T No. 3 waits to depart with the 5.55pm mixed train to Laxfield that includes three carriages previously operated by the Metropolitan Railway. Of the MSLR Hudswell Clarke locomotives, No. 3 was the last to be delivered, arriving at the railway in Spring 1909.
Copyright LCGB/Ken Nunn Collection

The MSLR station at Haughley closed in late 1939 after which services serving the former MSLR stations used a bay platform at the rear of the up platform of the main line Haughley station. In this view of Haughley, Class J15 0-6-0 No. 65447 is seen about to propel the stock of a train from Laxfield out of the bay platform. The site of the MSLR station is no longer discernible.
Copyright R.M. Casserley
Photographer H. C. Casserley

At Haughley on Wednesday 1st June 1936, apple green livery Class B12/3 4-6-0 No. 8559 leaves with an Ipswich - Norwich stopping train. Under British Railways this locomotive became No. 61559 and was scrapped in 1951.
Copyright LCGB/ Ken Nunn Collection

Class 31/4 A1A-A1A No. 5697 passes the remains of the down platform at Haughley with a mixed train in the early 1970s. The small notice on the porch type structure at the front of the former station building reads "Haughley Junction". No. 5697 was later renumbered 31419 and when the electric train heating equipment was isolated, became 31519. The locomotive was withdrawn in December 1995.

Photographer Dr. Ian C. Allen

At one time Haverhill had two stations, the earliest of these being that of the Colne Valley & Halstead Railway (CV&HR) which opened in 1863. This railway ran from Chappel to Haverhill via Halstead and had a junction at Chappel with the Great Eastern Railway (GER) from the outset, and from 1865 at Haverhill. Initially the CV&HR used their own station at Haverhill in Colne Valley Road, but this closed to passengers in 1924 after which all former CV&HR services used the GER Haverhill station in Station Road. The CV&HR route between Chappel and Haverhill was 5¼ miles shorter than that of the GER. For part of the time that the two Haverhill stations existed, the former CV&HR station was known as Haverhill South and the former GER station as Haverhill North. Apart from the CV&HR station at Haverhill and the section of track leading to it, the remainder of the CV&HR was in Essex. Following closure in 1924 to passengers, the former CV&HR Haverhill station was used as a goods depot and closed in April 1965. The former GER station closed completely in March 1967.

These scenes were recorded on Saturday 29th July 1911 and show two CV&HR locomotives constructed by Hawthorn, Leslie & Co. **Top** - CV&HR 2-4-2T No. 4 *Hedingham* shunting in the CV&HR goods yards at Haverhill. This locomotive, built in 1894, was withdrawn in September 1923 and not taken into LNER stock. **Bottom** - Passing a GER Class Y14 0-6-0 on a goods train, CV&HR 2-4-2T No. 3 *Colne* arrives at Haverhill from Chappel with a passenger train. Built in 1887, No. 3 became LNER Class F9 No. 8313 in July 1923 and was withdrawn in December 1927.
Photographs copyright LCGB/Ken Nunn Collection

CV&HR 2-4-2T No. 3 *Colne* comes off the Colne Valley line and passes Colne Valley Junction with the 1128am Chappel - Haverhill passenger service on Saturday 29th July 1911. Much of the rolling countryside in the background has now been given over to residential and industrial development. Part of the interconnecting line between the Stour Valley and Colne Valley lines, the viaduct in the distance still exists as the "Sturmer Arches". The Colne Valley line passed over this viaduct on the approach to Colne Valley Junction.
Copyright LCGB/Ken Nunn Collection

The GER station at Haverhill, seen here about 1910, closed in 1967 and was demolished in 1970. At one time, there were two signal boxes at Haverhill but one closed in the 1930s. Since this junction station and the railway lines serving it closed, there has been a substantial increase in the local population. In the past residents and others wishing to visit Cambridge or Colchester could have travelled by rail, but today road transport is the only form of travel available.
Copyright Lens of Sutton Association

In addition to carrying services between Ipswich and Cambridge via Newmarket, the railway west of Haughley Junction through Bury St. Edmunds forms part of an important cross country route from Ipswich to Peterborough and the Midlands. A number of stations on the line between Bury St. Edmunds and Ely have been closed including Higham which is seen here in 1950. The main station buildings were situated between the road bridge over the railway and the goods shed in the centre of the photograph. Both the former station buildings and goods shed still exists and are in use commercially.
Copyright HMRS/H. F. Hilton

Situated between Worlingworth and Wilby on the Mid Suffolk Light Railway, the station at Horham was in many respects similar to other stations on the line, a main building with a timber frame clad in corrugated iron, a smaller separate outbuilding and adjacent to a level crossing. This view is looking in the Laxfield direction and on the left is the goods siding. The final passenger service in 1952 consisted of two trains each way, one in the morning and the other in the afternoon with no Sunday service.
Courtesy Anglian Rail Archive

Ingham was one of the smaller Suffolk stations and is seen here on a postcard with a train arriving in August 1915. A typical weekday only service of just four trains each way was provided at Ingham. Travellers destined for London were usually advised to change at Bury St. Edmunds, Long Melford and Mark's Tey. Normally quite a quiet station, during both world wars Ingham was very busy. *Malcolm R. White Collection*

A few miles north of the Essex/Suffolk border in the 1930s, LNER Class B12/3 4-6-0 No. 8546 heads for Ipswich with a down express. Under British Railways this locomotive became No. 61546, and was allocated to Cambridge for two years prior to scrapping at Stratford in July 1959. *Courtesy Anglian Rail Archive*

An express headed by a GER Class S46 4-4-0, possibly from the second batch of these locomotives, about to enter Stoke Hill tunnel at Ipswich. *Copyright Lens of Sutton Collection*

The north end of Ipswich station with trains in all four platforms. Close examination of this scene shows a horse in the centre of the middle line between platforms 2 and 3. *Courtesy Past Times Prints*

This exterior view of Ipswich station shows how impressive the building looked before the seemingly ever increasing mass of "road furniture" became established on the station forecourt. This scene was recorded just before the Great War and well before items such as bus lanes, road islands and markings, crossings, traffic lights, advertisements and road signs became the norm in front of this fine building.
The now removed attractive bell housing complete with bell can be seen in the centre of the building. This station opened in 1860 and replaced the original one at Croft Street. *Courtesy Anglian Rail Archive*

This 1911 view of Ipswich station shows the same basic layout that we see today. One important difference is that the carriage sidings on the left are now used as a stabling point for freight locomotives and often diesel multiple units. Another is that the signal box in the left foreground (the London end of the island platform), was declared redundant and has been removed. The island platform was added by the GER in 1883.
Courtesy Anglian Rail Archive

On Monday 6th September 1909, oil fired Great Eastern Railway Class S46 4-4-0 No. 1900 *Claud Hamilton* is seen here heading the 10.00am London Liverpool Street - Felixstowe express on Ipswich troughs. Completed in 1900 and finished in the dignified Ultramarine Blue of the GER, *Claud Hamilton* visited France in 1900 where it was exhibited at the Paris Exhibition and won a gold medal.
As LNER Class D14 No. 2500, *Claud Hamilton* was withdrawn in May 1947 and the nameplates were transferred in August 1947 to D16/3 No. 2546 which had previously been GER No. 1855. As Class D16/3 4-4-0 No. 62546, this locomotive was withdrawn from service in mid 1957.
Copyright LCGB/Ken Nunn Collection

Complete with polished dome, builders plate and number plate, Mid Suffolk Light Railway (MSLR) locomotive No. 2, stands bunker to bunker with MSLR No. 3 at Ipswich sheds. When the LNER took over the MSLR in July 1924, they replaced the MSLR motive power with Class J65 0-6-0T locomotives. The Hudswell Clark built MSLR locomotives became Class J64 under the LNER coding system and No. 2 went on to become LNER No 8317 and was eventually scrapped in December 1929
Courtesy Anglian Rail Archive

During the mid 1930s and into the 1940s, a number of tank locomotives designed by J. G. Robinson and introduced in 1907 on the Great Central Railway, could be seen working from Ipswich, often on trains to Felixstowe. A number also worked from Bury St. Edmunds in the 1930s. LNER Class C14 4-4-2T No. 7447 was one of those transferred to former Great Eastern territory and here the locomotive is at Ipswich station on Saturday 28th June 1947. Locomotives of this class were similar to Class C13 locomotives which were introduced in 1903, but with a greater coal and water capacity.
Courtesy Anglian Rail Archive

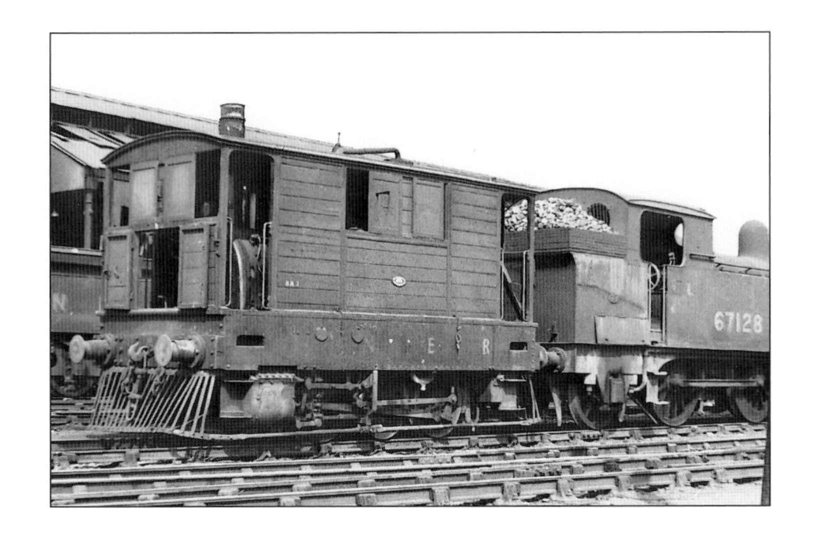

Locomotives on shed at Ipswich

Top Left - Unidentified Class J70 0-6-0T and Class F3 2-4-2T No. 67128 in early 1950. *Courtesy Alan Wood Collection*

Bottom Left - LNER Class J15 0-6-0 No. 7545 (later renumbered BR No. 65473) on 24th July 1938. *Copyright RCTS/CAS0025*

Top Right - Class B12/3 4-6-0 No. 61570 and Class B17/6 4-6-0 No. 61635 *Milton* on 28th April 1957. *Courtesy Anglian Rail Archive*

Bottom Right - LNER Class J67/2 0-6-0T No. 7013 (later renumbered BR No. 68518) on 24th July 1938. *Copyright RCTS/CAS0021*

Recalling the days when newspapers were distributed daily across the country by rail to hundreds of destinations, air braked fitted Class 03 0-6-0 No. 03399 (original number D2399) is seen at Ipswich with two newspaper vans.
Copyright Malcolm R. White

From the early 1940s when they were introduced, until the introduction of the "Britannia" Class 7MT 4-6-2 locomotives, a great deal of the mainline passenger work in Suffolk was entrusted to Thompson designed Class B1 4-6-0 locomotives. One of the 410 built, Stratford allocated No. 61373 is seen here at Ipswich in the early 1950s arriving at the up platform.
Copyright R.K. Blencowe Collection

The dock area of Ipswich has changed greatly in recent years with the railway no longer required on the majority of the waterfront, and many once familiar commercial buildings either demolished or converted for other uses. This scene, recorded on Saturday 20th June 1953, shows "Tram Loco" Class J70 0-6-0 No. 68219 on the waterfront and passing under the Cranfield Bros. building. An example of the atmospheric dockside gas lights can be seen on the right.
Today all the railway track in this area has either been covered over, removed or isolated as regeneration of the area moves forward.
Copyright RCTS/ FAI0293.

Another "Tram Loco", GER Class C53 0-6-0T (LNER Class J70), at work in Ipswich Docks. Recorded on Saturday 30th April 1910, GER No. 130 takes a break from shunting duties for the photographer. By 1955, these locomotives had been replaced at Ipswich by diesel locomotives such as Class DY1 0-4-0 No. 11150 and other types including Class DJ12 locomotives. An example of one of the last types of locomotives used around the dock area can be found in the colour section of this book.
Copyright LCGB/Ken Nunn Collection

Introduced by the GER in 1886, the Class J66 0-6-0T locomotives were designed by James Holden. One of the class, No. 68374 is seen at Ipswich engine sheds on Saturday 23rd July 1949.
Copyright Andrew C. Ingram

In contrast to most of the locomotive classes seen at Ipswich, the "Britannia" Class 7MT 4-6-2 locomotives were designed at Derby. Fifty-five of these fine locomotives were built and by July 1952, seven had been allocated to Stratford and eight to Norwich. One of the class, No. 70015 *Apollo*, is seen bursting out of the tunnel with a down express for Norwich in the early 1950s. At that time *Apollo* was allocated to Stratford depot.
Courtesy Anglian Rail Archive

The Gresley designed Class K3 2-6-0 three cylinder locomotives were an excellent mixed traffic type, equally able to haul heavy goods or express passenger trains. Several of these locomotives were allocated to local sheds including Lowestoft.
One of the class, No. 61908, is seen here at Ipswich with a passenger train that includes a fish van, a sight often seen on the railways of Suffolk. When working the fast Lowestoft - London fish trains, the capabilities of a certain Lowestoft footplate crew and "their" K3 became legendary since they often ran in front of the "Britannia" hauled expresses on their way to London.
Copyright David J. White

A 1957 scene at Ipswich with Class B12/3 4-6-0 No. 61549 having just arrived at platform two with a passenger train. Allocated to Stratford for many years, in late 1957 No. 61549 was reallocated to Cambridge. However the stay was short lived, for in January 1959 the locomotive was put in store at Stratford and scrapped there the following month. Introduced in 1932, the versatile Class B12/3 locomotives were Gresley rebuilds of S. D. Holden's design of 1911. Apart from the one example preserved on the North Norfolk Railway, the class was extinct by January 1960.
J.W.Sutherland/Foxline Publishing

Completed in the mid 1950s to replace the assortment of old buildings previously making up Ipswich sheds, this depot closed in 1968 and after being used for other purposes, the site was cleared and sold for residential development. *Courtesy Anglian Rail Archive*

A view in April 1954 of a very busy Lower Goods Yard at Ipswich with Class DJ12 0-6-0 No. 11141 at work in the yard. Officially closed and derelict by late 2009, the site may be sold to developers. *Copyright Essex Bus Enthusiasts Group/Photographer Frank Church*

The late afternoon of Saturday 26th May 1956 at Ipswich and Norwich allocated "Britannia" Class 7MT 4-6-2 No. 70030 *William Wordsworth* leaves with the down "*The Broadsman*" service. This ran between London Liverpool Street and Norwich and provided a through service to Wroxham, North Walsham Main, Cromer and Sheringham. At one time the train also stopped at Salhouse, Gunton and Worstead. A restaurant car was available between Cromer and London Liverpool Street. *Courtesy Anglian Rail Archive*

Above - With the end of steam traction on the main line through Ipswich, the top link duties of the "Britannia" class locomotives initially passed to English Electric Type 4 diesel electric locomotives. These were succeeded by the more successful Brush Type 4 diesel electric locomotives, an example of which is seen here arriving at Ipswich with a Norwich - London Liverpool Street express.
Copyright Malcolm R. White

Left - An Ipswich scene from 1985 with examples of Class 31, 37 and 47 diesel electric locomotives in the sidings adjacent to platform four. From left to right are No. 37057 (in store at time of writing), No. 37143 (in Spain), No. 31250 (scrapped 1995) and No. 47457 (scrapped 1992). With a few exceptions, diesel locomotives built in this country have largely been replaced on Britain's railways by locomotives built by foreign companies, examples of which can usually be seen today occupying these sidings.
Copyright Norman Fairhead

The two platform Kenton station was one of the more important Mid Suffolk Light Railway (MSLR) stations where a sizeable track layout existed. It was also where the short line to Debenham left the main MSLR Line; hopes that this would eventually reach Westerfield came to nothing. The typical MSLR station building and the unusual type of MSLR station nameboard are both well illustrated in this photograph. The large premises behind the station and wagons belonged to the local farmers' co-operative.
Courtesy Stations UK

In recent years Lakenheath has become known as one of the least used railway stations in the UK with trains only stopping there at weekends. This scene was recorded in 1915 when passenger numbers were greater and shows a train headed by a GER Class T19R 2-4-0 about to depart for Norwich.
The railway employee on the platform in the frock coat is possibly the station master. All the buildings seen here on both platforms have been demolished apart from the small brick building in the centre of the photograph.
Copyright HMRS/ H. F. Hilton

Only the bridge carrying the A1141 Bury Road on the far right of this photograph remains today as a reminder of the busy station and goods yard that once existed at Lavenham. This postcard shows the station, signal box, goods shed and the yard.
Malcolm R. White Collection

Within a short time of the Mid Suffolk Light Railway (MSLR) being absorbed in July 1924 by the LNER, the three MSLR Hudswell Clark locomotives were replaced by LNER Class J65 0-6-0 locomotives. At least eight of these J. Holden designed small tank locomotives worked on the former MSLR at different times over several years. One of these was LNER No. 7253 which is seen here "on shed" at Laxfield on Sunday 5th July 1936. Starting life as GER Class E22 No. 253, this locomotive was withdrawn in May 1949 as LNER No. 8215. Laxfield shed was a sub-shed of Ipswich.
Copyright R.M. Casserley
Photographer H.C. Casserley

The 3.25pm train for Haughley headed by LNER Class J65 0-6-0T No. 7157 is seen leaving Laxfield on Monday 1st June 1936. Having started life in 1889 as GER Class E22 No. 157, this locomotive was withdrawn from service in November 1947 as LNER No. 8212. Following the withdrawal from service of the Class J65 locomotives, motive power on the MSLR was provided by Class J15 0-6-0s, the light axle loading of these versatile machines making them most suitable for this railway.
Copyright LCGB/Ken Nunn

Leiston station opened in June 1859 as the terminus of the railway from Saxmundham but within a year the line had been extended to Aldeburgh. This view, from the platform at Leiston, is looking east and towards Aldeburgh. Although the level crossing still exists, the track has been simplified with just a single line now existing through what was the station platform to the Sizewell. siding and loop.
Copyright R.M. Casserley
Photographer H.C. Casserley

Looking west along the platform at Leiston on Monday 14th May 1956, as Class J15 0-6-0 No. 65447 arrives with the 5.56pm Saxmundham to Aldeburgh train. The tramway to the one time major engineering works of Richard Garrett and Sons Ltd. left the sidings behind the railway truck on the left. On the right is the goods shed complete with canopy.
Copyright R.M. Casserley
Photographer H.C. Casserley

A unique view of Leiston station from the footplate of the Richard Garrett works shunter *Sirapite* on Monday 14th May 1956. The track leading to the tramway and the works is on the right. *Sirapite* was built in 1906 by Aveling and Porter and was purchased by Richard Garrett and Sons in 1929. After being sold in the early 1960s, *Sirapite* was purchased by the Long Shop Museum and arrived back at Leiston in March 2004. After an extensive overhaul and restoration at the Museum this little locomotive was steamed in late 2009. The large object in the bottom centre of the photograph is *Sirapite*'s flywheel.
Copyright R. M. Casserley

Sirapite climbing up from the Main Street level crossing in the Garrett Town Works yard on Monday 14th May 1956. On the the smokebox door in brass, is the Garrett logo, not that of the builder Aveling and Porter! The water tower in the centre left was restored in 2002. *Copyright R. N. Casserley Photographer H. C. Casserley*

Sirapite at Station Road level crossing on Monday 14th May 1956. Leiston goods shed is in the background. *Copyright R. M. Casserley*

An immaculate *Sirapite* in Garrett's Station Works on Monday 14th May 1956. *Copyright R. M. Casserley / Photographer H.C. Casserley*

A scene at Leiston looking in the Saxmundham direction with Norwich allocated Class 31/0 A1A-A1A No. D5662 (later renumbered 31235) in the platform. This locomotive exists in preservation at the Mid Norfolk Railway. Recorded in the months leading up to closure of the station to passengers, a "Leiston" totem sign can be seen together with full signalling, complete trackwork and wagons in the siding. The railway through Leiston still exists to serve the nearby French owned nuclear power station, however this location bears little resemblance to that seen here in mid 1966.

Copyright Malcolm R. White
Photographer Dr. Ian C. Allen

A charming scene at the important junction station of Long Melford with 1912 built Class J15 0-6-0 No. 65464 having just arrived with a passenger train. Designed by T. W. Worsdell and introduced in 1883, this type of locomotive was a familiar sight in Suffolk and despite being a long established design, lasted almost to the end of steam traction in the county. Long Melford station building still exists as a well maintained property complete with station sign.
Copyright Essex Bus Enthusiasts Group
Photographer Frank Church

Just arriving at Long Melford on Friday 19th September 1952 is Class J15 0-6-0 No. 65438. This Cambridge allocated J15 was one of the class to be fitted with a tender cab to provide a more comfortable working environment for the driver and fireman when working tender first.
Copyright Mid Railway Trust, Ripley.

Cambridge allocated Ivatt LMS designed Class 4MT 2-6-0 No. 43149 in steam but derailed at Long Melford.
The Foxearth and District Local History Society

A view inside Long Melford Junction signal box. One of the gas lights is visible in the top left of the photograph.
The Foxearth and District Local History Society

Class D16/3 4-4-0 No. 62531 arrives at Long Melford with the 2.01pm Colchester - Cambridge train on Saturday 30th October 1954. Starting life in May 1903 as GER Class S46 4-4-0 No. 1860, No. 62531 was condemned on Saturday 21st March 1955 and scrapped at Stratford. There were a number of Class D16 derivatives and No. 62531 was a Gresley rebuild introduced in 1933 of Class D15/2 with a larger round topped boiler and modified footplating. Under the LNER this locomotive was No. 8860 and the actual rebuild date was June 1934.
Copyright LCGB/Ken Nunn Collection

The accounts of the Norfolk Railway and the Eastern Counties Railway show that vast sums of money were spent at Lowestoft between 1846 and 1855 in developing the railway and the harbour.

Top - The present Lowestoft railway station was completed in 1855 having been built by the Lucas Brothers. It replaced the original station that opened, initially for goods, with the railway to Reedham in May 1847. The line between Lowestoft and Reedham was built by the Norfolk Railway (NR) and the Lowestoft Railway and Harbour Company (LR&HC), with the NR operating the line from the outset. In 1846, the NR had been empowered to lease or purchase the LR&HC. In later years, the Eastern Counties Railway would take over from the NR. The station is seen here in 1912, with a GER omnibus waiting to depart for Southwold. In the foreground are a number of tracks, those running left to right being the Corporation tramway and in the bottom left of the photograph, are the railway lines from the station sidings to the network of lines around the docks. *Courtesy Peter Killby*

Bottom - This view of the north side of the station was recorded in 1905, when the station was in the ownership of the GER. The building at that time had not been subjected to the series of major changes that would follow in later years. These included the removal of the two towers on the entrance hall, the removal of the overall roof and the removal of the roof and track from platform one. The future of the station is uncertain at the time of writing (May 2010). A regeneration company and the local council wish to make substantial changes to the area around the station, and thereby release land for development and a new road. *Malcolm R. White Collection*

Great Eastern Railway (GER) Class M15R 2-4-2T No. 781 is seen here in 1905 leaving Lowestoft Central with a passenger train for Reedham. Completed in October 1904, it later became Class F5 2-4-2T No. 67194 and was withdrawn from service in October 1956. A new full size locomotive of this class is now being constructed by enthusiasts.
Courtesy Anglian Rail Archive

A fine sight at Lowestoft Central during the summer of 1920 as a GER Class S69 4-6-0 waits to return to London Liverpool Street with an officer's special. Designed by S. D. Holden for the GER, the first members of the class entered service in 1911. The majority of the class were built by the GER between 1911 and 1920 and others were built by W. Beardmore & Co., Glasgow in 1920 and 1921.
Courtesy Anglian Rail Archive

A view looking east from near Lowestoft signal box in the mid 1950s showing Class F6 2-4-2T No. 67231. One of the last two locomotives of this type at Lowestoft, No. 67231 left for scrapping in March 1958. In the early 1950s, representatives of Classes F3, F4, F5 and F6 could be found at Lowestoft covering a wide range of duties including passenger services to Beccles, Bungay and the Waveney Valley line, Yarmouth Beach, Yarmouth South Town and Reedham.
Courtesy Allan Wood Collection

To work trains to London Liverpool Street, Lowestoft was allocated a number of Class B17 4-6-0 locomotives. One of these was No. 61670 *City of London* which is seen here at Lowestoft engine shed. *City of London* was one of two Class B17/6 locomotives streamlined from 1937 until 1951. It was put into store at Stratford Works in March 1960 and scrapped there the following month.
Courtesy Allan Wood Collection

Locomotives on shed at Lowestoft in 1954.
Top Left - Class F5 2-4-2T No. 67214.
Bottom Left - Class K3 2-6-0 No. 61959.

All photographs copyright Norman Fairhead.
Top Right - Class J68 0-6-0T No. 68640.
Bottom Right - Class 7MT 4-6-2 No. 70037 *Hereward the Wake.*

A feature of the railway network at Lowestoft, were the tracks that crossed the A12 trunk road from the station sidings and Harbour Works to access the docks and the North Pier shingle/gravel grading mill. Chain driven locomotives built by the Sentinel Wagon Works were extensively used on these lines and also at the Inner Harbour sleeper depot. Departmental Locomotive No. 38 is seen here at work adjacent to the Trawl Dock in the 1950s. This Class Y3 0-4-0T was No. 68168 in BR stock and one of a number of Class Y1 and Y3 locomotives allocated to Lowestoft. They were preceded in this work by 0-4-0ST locomotives and succeeded by diesel shunters such as Class 03 0-6-0 Departmental No. 92. Petrol driven locomotives, road tractors and horses were also used at railway locations in the town for moving rolling stock.
Gresley Society/Malcolm R. White Collection

A number of three cylinder Class K3 2-6-0 locomotives were allocated to Lowestoft, mainly for use on fast goods traffic, but could also be seen handling heavy passenger traffic. One of these powerful machines was No. 61959, of which the interior of the cab is seen here in 1951 together with the regular crew of Driver George Freeman and Fireman Alfred Hubbard. This particular locomotive was maintained in superb condition by the crew and considered by many to be the cleanest and most highly polished in East Anglia. Unfortunately no examples of this versatile class were preserved.
Courtesy Alfred Hubbard

With its home shed on the left, Class K3/2 2-6-0 No. 61973 arrives at Lowestoft in the 1950s with a goods train containing many fish vans. On the far right can be seen the line to Yarmouth, at that time a busy rail link between the two coastal towns and serving Corton, Hopton and Gorleston, all popular with holidaymakers in the summer. On summer Saturdays, this and other local Class K3s, could be found working the "Holidays Camps Express" trains between Lowestoft and London. *Courtesy Alfred Hubbard*

BR Class Y1/1 0-4-0T No. 8130 was repainted in the Harbour Works paint shop with the result that those responsible received a reprimand for the style of lettering used by the enthusiastic works painters. With gleaming paintwork the Sentinel is seen here in the works yard with Driver Sydney Banks (in the centre) and two colleagues. Mr. Banks was a regular driver of the Sentinel locomotives and his duties included trips to the North Pier shingle/gravel grading mill and to the sleeper depot. The Class Y1/1 locomotives were introduced in 1925 and No. 8130 later became Departmental Locomotive No. 37. In the mid 1950s, No. 37 was broken up on the North Pier at Lowestoft, with the work being witnessed by the author. *Courtesy David J. White /Sydney Banks*

The Harbour Works were originally identified by a large sign proclaiming "North of Europe Steam Navigation Co. Engine Factory 1853". Later this sign was changed to "Great Eastern Railway Harbour Works 1853", followed by the "London & North Eastern Railway Harbour Works 1853". Eventually the works became a BR permanent way and concrete products depot. A complex track layout existed in and around the works with access to Town Quay, the network of lines around the Outer Harbour, and Lowestoft goods yard and sidings via a roadside track along Commercial Road and North Quay.

Top Left - Class 08 0-6-0 No. 08775 (original number D3943) trundles back to the main goods yard at Lowestoft along Commercial Road from the Harbour Works.

Top Right - A short train conveying concrete products and headed by a very smart Class O3 0-6-0 No. 03197 (original number D2197) is seen in Commercial Road on the track that gave access to the Harbour Works from the main goods yard and North Quay.
Both photographs copyright Malcolm R. White

Bottom Right - The works comprised a large yard and several buildings including that seen here with two GER vessels, the hopper barge *Mudsucker GER.* and behind that, the paddle tug *Despatch.*
Malcolm R. White Collection

Track recovery on the closed Lowestoft Central - Yarmouth South Town railway line in January 1971. **Top** - Looking south from Church Road towards Lowestoft Central with Lowestoft College on the left. **Bottom** - Looking north from Church Road towards St. Margaret's Road and Lowestoft North.
Both photographs copyright Malcolm R. White

Lowestoft BR Civil Engineering Harbour Works. **Top** - East end of the works yard showing some of the many buildings at this extensive engineering and concrete products facility. **Bottom** - A track maintenance vehicle ready to return to the national network after overhaul and repainting at the works. Conversion and maintenance of carriages and other rolling stock used in civil engineering was also carried out at the works.
Malcolm R. White Collection

The railway network at Lowestoft was vast and covered large areas in the centre and south of the town and along the north and south waterfronts around the harbour. The south waterfront was reached by a goods only branch from Oulton Broad South. One of the areas on the south waterfront was accessed via a track alongside Riverside Road which is where we find one of Lowestoft's Class 03 0-6-0 diesel shunters having just emerged from the Boulton & Paul factory. Unlike today with few true British cars on the road, here Austin, Hillman and Morris products complete the scene from the 1960s.

Copyright Malcolm R. White
Photographer Dr. Ian C. Allen

Above - An unidentified GER Class 209 (LNER Y5 0-4-0ST) is seen here at work on the North Pier. This location, where some of the sidings were on jetties over the North Sea, was a favourite haunt of the author in the 1950s.
Courtesy Anglian Rail Archive.
Top Left - Being close to the South Quay, the now closed goods depot in Belvedere Road in south Lowestoft was flooded on a number of occasions. This is the scene in January 1953.
Courtesy Peter Killby
Centre Left - Another January 1953 scene but showing the flooded railway cutting leading to Belvedere Road goods depot. The cutting is now part of a cycle way and foot path.
Courtesy Peter Killby
Bottom Left - The Mill Road bridge from which the two scenes of flooding were recorded in 1953. Lowestoft's Class J15 0-6-0 No. 65478 is in the cutting with a goods train having just left the goods yard. *Malcolm R. White Collection*

Perhaps because of the two routes to the town, railtour operators have long favoured Lowestoft as a destination for special steam and diesel hauled trains resulting in a wide variety of motive power appearing at Lowestoft Central. One such railtour was on Saturday 10th February 1990 and featured an HST125 (High Speed Train). The train is seen arriving at Lowestoft headed by Class 43 Power Car No. 43073 with Power Car No. 43154 at the rear. Introduced in 1977, the power cars were fitted with a Paxman Valenta 12RP200L engine producing 2250bhp at 1500rpm with electrical equipment supplied by Brush. Both power cars was built for use in the 254 series of units allocated to East Coast main line services.
Copyright Norman Fairhead

Class 55 "Deltic" No. 55015 *Tulyer* is one of hundreds of former BR diesel powered locomotives now preserved and cared for by enthusiasts. This impressive machine visited Lowestoft on Sunday 3rd September 1978 with a railtour from London Kings Cross via Cambridge and Norwich, and returned via Ipswich and Cambridge. The Class 55 is seen here waiting for the passengers to return to the train for the journey back to Kings Cross. *Tulyer* was withdrawn from service in January 1982 and is now one of three of these machines owned by the Deltic Preservation Society. On the right is a carriage of the set used on the Lowestoft Central - London Liverpool Street (Sundays excepted) through train.
Copyright Norman Fairhead

Built by Beyer, Peacock & Co. Ltd. in 1888 and later fitted with a Midland boiler, M&GN Class A 4-4-0 No. 32 is seen here with a train from Yarmouth Beach at Lowestoft North in 1936. *Courtesy J. C Thorne/Anglian Rail Archive*

The "Holiday Camps Express" from London Liverpool Street approaches Lowestoft North headed by Class D16/3 4-4-0 No. 62613. The first stop on this busy coast line was Corton, which had several holiday parks in or near the village. *Copyright David J. White*

Class D16/3 4-4-0 No. 62546 *Claud Hamilton* leaves Lowestoft North with a Yarmouth South Town - Lowestoft Central train. This view is from the bridge carrying the A12 road over the railway, and shows the Camping Coach, station and yard. *Copyright SLS*

Lowestoft North closed with the Lowestoft Central - Yarmouth South Town railway line in 1970. This view is looking north in the early 1960s when goods traffic, mainly coal and sometimes bricks, was still handled at the station. *Courtesy Anglian Rail Archive*

The Wickham Market - Framlingham railway line crossed the A12 London - Great Yarmouth trunk road immediately west of Marlesford station. In this postcard, published when the station was operated by the Great Eastern Railway, the level crossing gates for the road can be seen between the signal box and the platform end. Today the former station building is a well maintained private residence.
Malcolm R. White Collection

The station at Mellis closed in 1966 and at one time had been the junction for the branch to the nearby town of Eye. Mellis is seen here after closure and before the electrification of the main line between Norwich and Ipswich. An express headed by a Class 47 Co-Co diesel electric locomotive passes through the disused station and past Mellis Junction signal box. The platform once used by trains to Eye is on the right and behind the signal box.
Copyright Malcolm R. White

Recorded in the days of the Great Eastern Railway, this view of Mellis station shows a train for Eye in the branch platform and a stopping train on the main line about to depart for Ipswich.
It seems the lad standing on the ladder in the bottom centre of the photograph had been forewarned that the scene was being recorded by the photographer.
Courtesy Anglian Rail Archive

A comprehensive view of Melton station in the 1930s when it was operated by the London & North Eastern Railway (LNER) showing a wealth of details, most of which are missing today. Visible are both platforms, LNER station furniture, some of the gardens, the signal box, the goods shed and on the down line a train headed by an unidentified Class J15 0-6-0 complete with LNER number on the buffer beam.
Courtesy Past Times Publishing

An interesting scene at Melton with Class 37/0 Co-Co No. 37051 involved in shunting, and on the left a small privately owned shunter. The station can just be seen in the distance near the level crossing gates and on the right is Melton signal box. Originally No. D6751, this Class 37/0 was withdrawn from service in March 2004 and later cut up at Beeston
Copyright Malcolm R. White
Photographer Dr. Ian C. Allen.

Class 31/1 A1A-A1A Nos. 31158 and 31233 with a stone train at Melton during the 1970s. Locomotive No. 31158 was withdrawn in 1994 and No. 31233 remains active on the national rail network at the time of writing.
Copyright Malcolm R. White
Photographer Dr. Ian C. Allen

The corrugated iron-clad timber framed buildings at Mendlesham were typical of those found at stations on the Mid Suffolk Light Railway. In this view of the station, the larger building consisted of a booking office, an open waiting shelter in the centre, and a store room. The smaller building contained the Gentlemen's toilet and a store.
Mendlesham had a loop west of the station with a short siding to the loading bay. This view is looking towards the next station of Brockford & Wetheringsett which was just 1½ miles further east, whilst the end of the line for passengers was 14½ miles away at Laxfield. To the west, Haughley station and the main line connection was 4½ miles.
Copyright Lens of Sutton Association

The majority of the railway to Mildenhall was in the county of Cambridgeshire, but Mildenhall itself is in Suffolk. In LNER days, J. Holden designed LNER Class E4 2-4-0 No. 7441 waits to leave the Suffolk town with a Cambridge train. This scene appears to have been recorded in 1933, when No. 7441 was briefly allocated to Cambridge. In June 1937, this locomotive was condemned.
Courtesy Past Times Publishing

The view from the platform at Mildenhall looking towards Worlington Golf Links Halt which was 1 mile away. In the early 1950s, the first train of the day which called at all ten stations, left Mildenhall at 7.45am and took 60 minutes to reach Cambridge. A turntable was installed at Mildenhall and this was located behind the signal box on the left.
Courtesy Anglian Rail Archive

The scene at Mildenhall on Saturday 16th June 1962 as the final passenger train prepares to depart for Cambridge complete with a headboard with the slogan "A merciful release after a long illness". The train is a Class 109 Wickham diesel multiple unit, one example of which has been preserved and can be seen (2010) at the Llangollen Railway. At one time the "final train" on a doomed railway line seemed not unusual in Suffolk as the network was tailored to being more cost effective and meeting present day apparent needs.
Copyright T. Middlemass / Andrew C. Ingram

Needham Market was opened in late 1846 by the Ipswich, Bury and Norwich Railway Company as Needham. The splendid Jacobean style building was designed by Frederick Barnes and built by Stowmarket contractor Daniel Revett.
The station, which is now located between Ipswich and Stowmarket, closed in 1967. However, in 1971 it reopened as unstaffed Needham Market.

Top - The main station building at Needham Market on Tuesday 20th August 1968 . This splendid Grade II structure was restored in 2000 and is on the down side of the station. Since being built, it has been altered and at one time had Dutch gables and ogee caps on the towers. At the time of writing, Needham Market is served by services between Ipswich, Ely and Cambridge.
Copyright RCTS/LUL3412

Bottom - The station at Needham Market in the early 1920s as seen from track level and looking in the Ipswich direction. This view shows the signal box complete with signalman and a fine floral display, both platforms and an assembly of station staff. Also visible is one of the attractive chimneys and some of the Dutch gables of the station building.
Copyright Lens of Sutton Association

Very few East Anglian towns and cities can match the number of stations that have served Newmarket since the railway first reached the town. Seen here is the first station building that opened with the line from Chesterford in 1848. An island platform was added in 1879 to cope with additional services.
This station was replaced in 1902 by a larger Great Eastern Railway (GER) built station sited further south. The 1848 building continued in railway use initially to support the racing industry and later as a goods station.

Despite being considered as "listed", this impressive structure was demolished in 1980 to make way for residential development.

Top - The imposing external frontage in 1950. *Copyright HMRS/H. F. Hilton collection*

Bottom - An internal view in 1950. *Copyright HMRS/H. F. Hilton collection*

The 1879 island platform at Newmarket was joined to the 1848 terminus platform by a footbridge. With the opening in 1902 of the GER built station, the island platform became disused, but the original single platform was retained for traffic associated with the racing industry. This scene was recorded on Wednesday 4th August 1909 and shows GER Class T19 2-4-0 No. 738 passing the disused remains of the island platform with the 4.12pm Cambridge - Ipswich train.
Copyright LCGB/Ken Nunn Collection

The new station at Newmarket is seen here as GER Class N31 0-6-0 No. 547 passes through with the 5.20pm Newmarket - Cambridge goods train on Wednesday 4th August 1909. The Class N31 locomotives were a disappointment and the GER started to withdraw the class in 1908. Built in 1897, No. 547 was withdrawn in 1911. As their Class J14, the London & North Eastern Railway continued to withdraw the remaining locomotives from service with the last being condemned in 1925. One of the problems with this design was the positioning of the steam chest and the valves. These were positioned below the cylinders leading to the steam chest becoming waterlogged and restricting the airflow to the ashpan. The class became known for the very sluggish performance.
Copyright LCGB/Ken Nunn Collection

Class B12/3 4-6-0 No. 61562 arrives with a Ipswich - Cambridge train in the early 1950s at the GER built station at Newmarket. Completed at Stratford in April 1920 as GER Class S69 No. 1562, this locomotive was withdrawn from service in August 1955.
Courtesy Anglian Rail Archive

Located in the north of Newmarket, the station at Warren Hill was used primarily by those associated with the horse racing industry. This view is from the platform of Warren Hill and shows the 2.30pm Haughley - Cambridge train about to enter Warren Hill tunnel on Wednesday 4th August 1909. The train is hauled by GER Class M15 2-4-2T No. 793 which was condemned in August 1923, and scrapped at Stratford. Under the LNER, some of the GER Class M15 locomotives became Class F4 and others, which had been either rebuilt or reboilered, became F5.
Copyright LCGB/Ken Nunn Collection

Orwell is one of many Suffolk stations no longer in existence, having been closed in 1955. One of the original stations on the railway built in 1877 between Westerfield and Felixstowe, this view of Orwell is looking in the Felixstowe direction was recorded on Monday 14th May 1956.
Copyright R.M. Casserley
Photographer H.C. Casserley

Oulton Broad North is adjacent to the junction where the Lowestoft - Norwich and Ipswich lines separate. In this view, looking east towards Lowestoft, the Ipswich line can be seen curving away to the right. In the days when rail services were more tailored to the needs of the passenger, the Lowestoft - York through train arrives at Oulton Broad North up platform headed by an unidentified 800hp British Thomson Houston /Clayton Bo-Bo Type 1 (later Class 15). Visible on the right are Esso fuel tankers on a siding associated with a now closed fuel depot. Lowestoft once had a number of long distance through services to various destinations. The last of these was to London, and in 2010 the Labour Government agreed to their withdrawal, despite them being very popular with users of the East Suffolk Line and, consequently, often full.
Copyright Stuart Jones

Top Right - Class L1 2-6-4T locomotives were allocated to a number of East Anglian locations. In Suffolk, Ipswich and Lowestoft were both home sheds to examples of these powerful locomotives. Lowestoft allocated No. 67707 is seen here involved in shunting at Oulton Broad North in 1958. *Copyright M. W. Knight / Andrew C. Ingram*

Oulton Broad North is a well used station on the Lowestoft - Norwich line serving a large residential area west of Lowestoft and close to areas destined for future housing schemes. A busy level crossing exists adjacent to the station.

Bottom Left - A view showing the demolished waiting rooms on the platforms. **Bottom Right** - The view of the station prior to demolition of the footbridge and replacement of the gates with barriers. *Both photographs copyright Stuart Jones.*

Oulton Broad North level crossing gates were replaced by barriers and the footbridge was removed in the 1970s. *Copyright Peter Calvert*

Another view of the footbridge removal. Now heritage railways are often eager to purchase these structures. *Copyright Peter Calvert*

Class J15 0-6-0 No. 65435 approaches Oulton Broad North junction on the way back to Lowestoft main goods yard, after working on the complex of railway lines and sidings on the south waterfront and in south Lowestoft. *Courtesy Peter Calvert*

Once owned by S. Swonnell and Son, the maltings at Oulton Broad had rail access from the North station via a long siding. This scene shows a truck being taken across Caldecott Road to the maltings, which are now converted for residential use. *Courtesy Peter Calvert*

A view from the footbridge at Oulton Broad North of Norwich allocated Class D16/3 4-4-0 No. 62619 passing the site of Mutford station on the approach to Oulton Broad North with a van train destined for Lowestoft. This scene was recorded by the author during the afternoon of Saturday 30th March 1957 On Monday 7th October 1957, No. 62619 was condemned and later scrapped at Stratford.
Copyright Malcolm R. White

Oulton Broad South is shrouded in fog as an Ipswich service worked by a Class 101 Metropolitan-Cammell diesel multiple unit arrives at the station. In the 1960s, many of these services originated at Yarmouth South Town. For example, in 1965 the 0615hrs departure from Yarmouth South Town would depart from Oulton Broad South at 0647hrs and arrive at Ipswich at 0802hrs. The station now has a single platform with the down line (on the left) recovered in the mid 1980s, the building on the down platform is now a hair dressing salon and the former main station building on the up platform is now a private residence. Where the Pullman Camping Coach is standing behind the down platform, is now a private car park.
Courtesy Peter Killby

The view looking east from the bridge seen in the previous photograph and showing the goods line to south Lowestoft leaving the Ipswich - Lowestoft line, and also Oulton Broad South Junction signal box. The goods line served Kirkley goods depot, Belvedere Road goods depot and a number of rail connected businesses, some of which were on the south Inner Harbour waterfront. An earlier signal box and a siding, were at one time located in the bottom right corner of the photograph. This scene was recorded by the author in 1972, the year the line finally closed.
Copyright Malcolm R. White

After crossing to the other side of the bridge, this was the view looking down on the station and west towards Beccles. Much has changed since this scene was recorded including the recovery of the down line and the disposal of the down platform and the building. Oulton Broad South is located near to the Broad with various leisure related parks and attractions nearby. It is also set in a large residential area for which further housing schemes are being promoted by various developers. The vacant land seen here to the west of the main station building is now fully occupied by housing.
This station is one of those set to lose the London through service as agreed by the Labour Government in early 2010.
Copyright Stuart Jones

The railway station at Parham was located in the centre of the village and just off the B1116 road. Opening in June 1859, Parham station was busiest during World War II when a large air base was built nearby for the United States 8th Army Air Force. Building materials were handled at the station and following the opening of the base in the summer of 1943, the station received large consignments of fuel and bombs for the USAAF. Parham is seen here during the period when it was open for goods traffic only.
Copyright Stuart Jones

Raydon was one of the stations on the Bentley - Hadleigh branch line and opened, unfinished, to goods traffic in August 1847 and to passengers the following month. In 1895, the station was renamed Raydon Wood. This view is looking east towards Capel in the early 1960s. Raydon Wood closed to passengers in February 1932 and to goods traffic in April 1965.
Malcolm R. White Collection

A view looking towards Bury St. Edmunds from the up platform at Saxham & Risby, one of the stations on the cross country route linking Ipswich with Cambridge, Ely and the Midlands that closed in 1967. On the up platform a small waiting shelter, the canopy of which is just visible on the right, a toilet and the signal box were located. The railway at this location was built by the Newmarket & Chesterford Railway and opened in 1854. It was operated by the Eastern Counties Railway from the outset.
Courtesy Anglian Rail Archive

Complete with oil lamps, the main station building at Saxmundham station whilst in Great Eastern Railway ownership is the subject of this unusual postcard. A fine collection of horse drawn carriages have converged on the station to await the arrival of a train. The building remains essentially the same today.
Malcolm R. White Collection

A comprehensive view of Saxmundham on Monday 14th May 1956 showing several features no longer seen there including the bay platform on the left, a train in the now demolished down platform, the footbridge, and sidings on the right. Track occupies the location of the present down platform
Copyright R. M. Casserley
Photograper H.C. Casserley

Class J15 0-6-0 No. 65447 passes the goods shed at Saxmundham on Monday 14th May 1956 with the 7.24pm Saxmundham - Aldeburgh passenger train.
Copyright/photographer R. M. Casserley

The view from the now demolished down platform at Saxmundham on Friday 16th September 1966 as an unidentified Class 37 Co-Co diesel locomotive leaves with the 7.18am Lowestoft - London Liverpool Street through train. This platform was replaced by a shorter one opposite the main station building and the up platform. The footbridge has also been demolished. *Courtesy Anglian Rail Archive*

Much of the former Aldeburgh branch line has been retained to access the sidings, gantry and loading facilities associated with the French owned nuclear power station at Sizewell. The sidings, which are on the south side of King George's Avenue at Sizewell level crossing, are seen here together with a train loaded with four flasks used to transport nuclear material. *Copyright Malcolm R. White*

The goods only branch to the sidings and maltings at Snape opened in 1859 and was just 1½ miles in length. The line was intended to carry passengers and indeed in the 1868 National Gazetteer, Snape is shown as a passenger station on the East Suffolk Railway. However the passenger service never materialised and the branch was used for goods traffic until March 1960. This typical scene shows class J15 0-6-0 No. 65388 at Snape sidings with part of the maltings in the background. The goods shed can be seen behind the lorry in the centre right
Courtesy Allan Wood Collection

From the sidings at Snape the railway crossed the B1069 road to enter the maltings complex. This view is looking west and shows the railway tracks crossing the road. The goods shed mentioned in the previous caption can be seen on the left.
Courtesy Past Times Prints

The Railway Enthusiasts Club **railtour - Sunday 30th September 1956**

All photographs copyright Richard M. Casserley

The railtour at Snape Junction signal box with passengers leaving the train by methods frowned upon today.

Lowestoft's Class E4 2-4-0 No. 62797 provided the motive power to Snape. Built in 1902, No. 62797 was condemned in March 1958.

No. 62797 looks superb at Snape in the autumn sunshine as onlookers witness this unique event on the normally goods only line.

On the return journey, assistance was provided by Ipswich's Class J15 0-6-0 No. 65447. This view is from the signal box and shows the train approaching the junction with the East Suffolk line.

The station at Somerleyton is close to the Norfolk/Suffolk border and today the station building is in use as a private residence. A number of other features of Somerleyton have changed over the years including on the down platform, the removal of the canopy on the main building, and the small wooden building. On up platform, the signal box and the canopied shelter have also been removed with passengers now being provided with bus-stop type shelters on both platforms. This view shows the station staff on the down platform in 1950. Somerleyton Hall and the village are reasonably close to the station, which was constructed in a mock Elizabethan style.
Copyright HMRS/H. F. Hilton

A short distance west of Somerleyton station is the swing bridge that takes the railway over the River Waveney and into Norfolk. This unusual view is from Somerleyton Marshes and shows a Metropolitan-Cammell Class 101 diesel multiple unit forming a Lowestoft - Norwich service crossing the bridge. The diesel multiple unit carries the Regional Railways livery. *Copyright Peter Calvert*

A number of passenger services provided by the Great Eastern Railway (GER) involved the use of motor omnibuses. One of these was between Lowestoft and Southwold, where GER omnibus No. 3 (BJ205) is seen in the Market Place. According to the local newspaper the service commenced on Monday 18th July 1904 with the buses making three return journeys a day between Lowestoft and Southwold each taking 1hr 40minutes. The service was withdrawn in 1913 due to competition from another larger omnibus operator.
Malcolm R. White Collection

On the 3ft. gauge Southwold Railway, Sharp Stewart 2-4-2T No. 1 *Southwold* waits to depart from Southwold with a mixed train for Halesworth. This locomotive was the second to carry the name *Southwold.* Due to financial reasons, in 1883 the first No. 1 had been returned to the builders who resold it to a customer in Colombia after converting the gauge to 3ft. 6inches. The locomotive seen here was delivered in 1893 when the financial position of the railway had improved and the two locomotives then on the railway, No. 2 *Halesworth* and No. 3 *Blyth,* were dealing with a greater volume of traffic. This No. 1 was scrapped in May 1929 at Southwold.
Courtesy Malcolm Maclean Archive

This view is of the approach to Southwold station early in the 20th century with a carriage standing at the location where a carriage shed was constructed and in use by 1903. In the centre of the photograph is the station building and immediately to the left of this is the engine shed. Several alterations and additions were made to the station over the years including enlargement of the station building, additional sidings, the installation of electric lights and the construction of toilets and a bookstall. The present day Blyth Hotel is under construction in the background, this was originally the Station Hotel and has also been known as the Pier Avenue Hotel.
Courtesy Malcolm Maclean Archive

One of three locomotives supplied to the railway in 1879 for the opening of the railway, Sharp Stewart 2-4-0T No. 3 *Blyth* is seen here shunting goods trucks at Southwold.
Courtesy Malcolm Maclean Archive

Almost the last day of the Southwold Railway and staff and employees pose with one of the original Sharp Stewart locomotives to mark the occasion. The last train was hauled by No. 4 *Wenhaston*, a powerful Manning, Wardle 0-6-2T that was new in 1914. *Courtesy Stanley Earl*

Situated between Clare and Sturmer in Cambridgeshire, Stoke station was also known as Stoke by Clare in addition to Stoke (Suffolk), the name it was officially given between 1932 and 1965. Stoke is seen here in 1950, and following closure in 1967, the station building was converted into a private residence and considerably extended.
Copyright HMRS/H. F. Hilton

Seventeen days after this scene was recorded at Stowmarket, Class B1 4-6-0 No. 61057 would be condemned following a collision that rendered the locomotive uneconomic to repair. It was the first of the class to be scrapped. This Saturday 18th February 1950 scene shows No. 61057 passing Stowmarket with an Ipswich bound passenger train.
Copyright Andrew C. Ingram

English Electric "Deltic" Class 55 Co-Co No. 9012 *Crepello* was an unusual visitor to Stowmarket on Sunday 17th May 1970 whilst working train 1Z20, a railtour from Leeds to Diss organised by the RCTS. This Type 5 locomotive, later to become No. 55012, is seen here running round the train. Introduced in 1961 and powered by two 18cyl. Napier "Deltic" engines of 1,650hp each and six English Electric traction motors, it was uncommon to see this type in Suffolk apart from whilst working railtours. Entering service in September 1961, *Crepello* was withdrawn in May 1981 and broken up in September the same year.
Copyright Malcolm R. White
Photographer John Ashley

Class 37/0 Co-Co No. 37026 (original number D6726) and Class 31/1 A1A-A1A No. 31317 (original number D5851) pass with caution construction work being carried out as part of a major road building project at Stowmarket.
Copyright Malcolm R. White
Photographer Dr. Ian C. Allen

This view at Stowmarket shows the station entrance and the north wing of this grand building. Complete with tower, a south wing similar to the north wing but in reverse, exists to the right of the station entrance where a number of railway staff and several passengers are assembled. This elaborate and much acclaimed structure was the work of Frederick Barnes. An extensive restoration project on this listed building was completed in May 1987 by British Railways and the Railway Heritage Trust.
Malcolm R. White Collection

Shortly after the opening of the Mid Suffolk Light Railway (MSLR) to passengers on Tuesday 29th September 1908, Hudswell Clark 0-6-0T No. 1 is seen at Stradbroke with the stock of a special working comprising six wheeled Great Eastern Railway passenger coaches. At the time this scene was recorded, the MSLR used four wheeled coaches for normal passenger services.
Copyright MSLR Archive

At one time it seemed that Sudbury would be removed from the railway map altogether, but today it remains open as an unstaffed terminus station with basic facilities and a much admired garden. These scenes were recorded in the 1950s when it was an intermediate station on the important cross country route between Colchester, Haverhill and Cambridge that closed in 1967. These scenes feature three locomotive types that originated from the Great Eastern Railway and examples of all three exist today.
Top left - Class J17 0-6-0 No. 65520 pauses near Sudbury Goods signal box whilst involved in shunting as an unidentified Class B12/3 4-6-0 arrives at Sudbury with a Colchester - Cambridge passenger train. **Top Right** - Later the same day, No. 65520 leaves Sudbury with a mixed goods train. This J17 was built in 1901 and is seen here fitted with a tender cab for better weather protection for the driver and fireman. **Bottom Right** - Sudbury has had stations in three different locations. The building seen here was the second which was demolished in 1986 to make way for redevelopment. This was replaced by the present modern unstaffed basic station. In this view of Sudbury, Class E4 2-4-0 No. 62785 waits to leave with a Cambridge - Colchester passenger train.
Copyright Essex Bus Enthusiasts Group / Photographer Frank Church

A rather different and now totally unrecognisable view of Sudbury with diesel electric locomotive Class 31/1 A1A-A1A No. D5659 (later renumbered 31232) standing on the line to the goods shed whilst shunting in the yard. The interesting tanker on the right is a bulk flour container wagon, this is standing with the box van on the line that at one time went to the small single road engine shed, the cattle pens and passed by the railway stables. The original 1849 passenger station at Sudbury became part of the goods facilities when a new station was opened in 1865. Dominating the background is the Church of St. Peter. This building was declared redundant in 1972 and is now in the care of The Churches Conservation Trust.

Copyright Malcolm R. White
Photographer Dr. Ian C. Allen

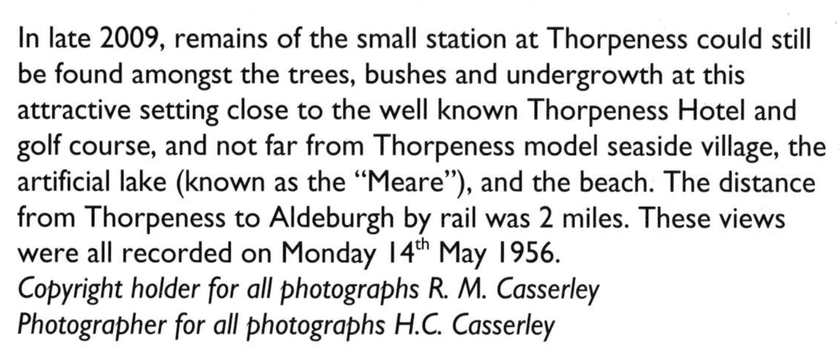

In late 2009, remains of the small station at Thorpeness could still be found amongst the trees, bushes and undergrowth at this attractive setting close to the well known Thorpeness Hotel and golf course, and not far from Thorpeness model seaside village, the artificial lake (known as the "Meare"), and the beach. The distance from Thorpeness to Aldeburgh by rail was 2 miles. These views were all recorded on Monday 14th May 1956.
Copyright holder for all photographs R. M. Casserley
Photographer for all photographs H.C. Casserley

Top Left - A view of the platform from a train arriving at Thorpeness from Saxmundham. **Top Right** - A platform view looking towards Aldeburgh with the goods siding on the right. **Bottom Left** - Passengers leave the platform having just alighted from a Saxmundham - Aldeburgh train. The three carriage bodies were used to provide passenger facilities. **Bottom Right** - Class J15 0-6-0 No. 65447 leaves Thorpeness with an Aldeburgh bound train and provides us with this pleasant view of the Suffolk coastal countryside.

Class F6 2-4-2T No. 67220 arrives at Thorpeness with an afternoon Aldeburgh - Saxmundham passenger train in July 1952. Designed by S. D. Holden for the Great Eastern Railway (GER), the Class F6 locomotives were a development of the Class F4 with a higher boiler pressure and greater water capacity. No. 67220 was completed by the GER in April 1911 and withdrawn from service in July 1955. *Courtesy Allan Wood Collection*

An unusual view of Thorpeness from amongst the vegetables in the station garden. This station was particularly popular in the summer months and being situated adjacent to a level crossing on the B1353 road, was easy to access. *Malcolm R. White Collection*

Thurston was known for the fine Barnes designed station buildings, with that on the down platform surviving today but not in railway use. This view is looking towards Elmswell with on the right, the now demolished up platform building. *Courtesy Anglian Rail Archive*

Passengers waiting at Walberswick station in the early 1900s. The station had two sidings and was situated approximately a ½ mile from the village. *Courtesy Malcolm Maclean Collection*

Trains conveying hundreds of containers now pass through Trimley each week. This view of the station, looking in the Felixstowe direction, was recorded in quieter times and shows a Metropolitan-Cammell Class 101 diesel multiple unit forming an Ipswich - Felixstowe service approaching the down platform.
The station building on the up platform (on the right) was demolished many years ago and the unused platform is now derelict and overgrown. The loop has been removed but part of the formation now forms the access leading to Felixstowe North Terminal with this line, once clear of the up platform, heading south east across the fields to the docks. Changes in the track layout near Trimley are planned as part of the Felixstowe Docks railway access improvement project which is mentioned elsewhere in this book. *Courtesy Anglian Rail Archive*

A mixed train hauled by the 1879 built 2-4-0T No. 2 *Halesworth* passes through the woods on the section of track between Walberswick and Blythburgh stations. *Malcolm Maclean Collection*

The station at Wenhaston was between Halesworth and Blythburgh on the narrow gauge Southwold Railway. This view is of Sharp Stewart 2-4-2T No. 1 *Southwold* approaching Wenhaston with a heavy up train in July 1920. Entering service in 1893, this locomotive replaced the previous *Southwold* that left the railway in 1883. Unlike the first locomotive of the same name and number which had the 2-4-0 wheel arrangement, this No. 1 had a pair of trailing wheels giving smoother running. *Courtesy Malcolm MacLean collection*

The former station building at Welnetham has now been extended and serves as a private residence with the track bed filled in to platform level, to create a lawn. Class J15 0-6-0 No. 65461 is seen at the station in the 1950s working a Bury St. Edmunds - Long Melford train. *Copyright Paul Anvil*

Wilby was set in a somewhat remote location, the main station building consisting of a timber framed corrugated iron clad hut with extra storage space being provided by a grounded van body. This station opened later than others on the Mid Suffolk Light Railway and was considered the least used on the line. *Copyright Stations UK.*

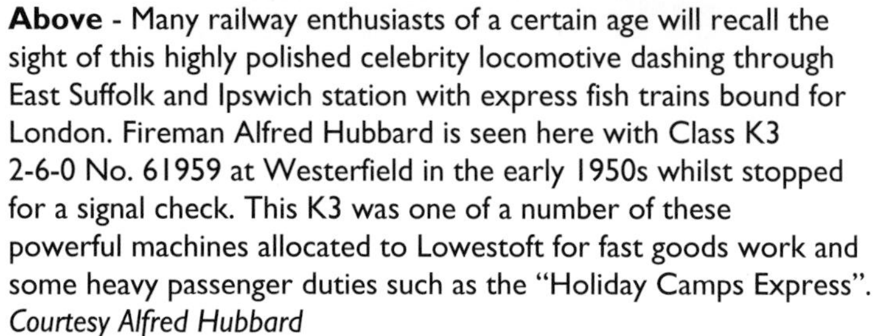

Above - Many railway enthusiasts of a certain age will recall the sight of this highly polished celebrity locomotive dashing through East Suffolk and Ipswich station with express fish trains bound for London. Fireman Alfred Hubbard is seen here with Class K3 2-6-0 No. 61959 at Westerfield in the early 1950s whilst stopped for a signal check. This K3 was one of a number of these powerful machines allocated to Lowestoft for fast goods work and some heavy passenger duties such as the "Holiday Camps Express". *Courtesy Alfred Hubbard*

Top Right - The original layout at Westerfield is seen here with the Felixstowe Railway & Pier Company (FR&PC) terminal station on the left, and the Great Eastern Railway platforms on the right. *Courtesy Anglian Rail Archive*

Bottom Right - Looking smart whilst in use by British Railways in the 1950s, this is a closer view of the FR&PC station at Westerfield. With flower beds on the platform, flower pots by the track, on the building and the buffers, obviously the staff took great pride in their working environment that included maintaining the large white Westerfield sign bordered by trimmed grass on the left. At the time of writing the area seen here occupied by track has become home to a range of trees, bushes and plants. *Copyright Lens of Sutton*

This view of Wickham Market in June 1962 shows the station before the modernisation of the East Suffolk line and the removal of surplus infrastructure and track. On the right beyond the station building is the goods shed. *Copyright Stuart Jones*

The platforms at Wickham Market were staggered and the up platform and the shelter, which is seen here in November 1978, were demolished as part of the modernisation.
Malcolm R. White Collection

For several years Class 24 Bo-Bo diesel locomotives were allocated to Ipswich and became a familiar sight in the county. Class member No. D5037 is seen passing Wickham Market in 1966 with a summer Saturday express for Lowestoft and Yarmouth South Town. On Saturdays in the summer, Yarmouth South Town had ten of these trains from London Liverpool Street via Lowestoft and the East Suffolk line. Introduced in 1958 and built by Beyer Peacock and British Railways, Class 24 locomotives were powered by a Sulzer 6 Cyl. 6LDA28 engine producing 1,160bhp at 750rpm. Four Class 24 locomotives are preserved, but D5037 (later renumbered 24037) was scrapped.
Copyright Malcolm R. White
Photographer Dr. Ian C. Allen

An early evening scene between Wickham Market and Saxmundham as Class 31/1 A1A-A1A No. 31151 heads for Lowestoft with a passenger train from London Liverpool Street. This locomotive originally carried the number D5569 and was withdrawn from service in October 1986, having at one time been allocated to Norwich (32A).
Copyright Malcolm R. White
Photographer Dr. Ian C. Allen

The footbridge at Woodbridge provided an excellent vantage point to record this scene showing Ipswich allocated Class B1 4-6-0 No. 61059 about to leave with a down train for Lowestoft and Yarmouth. Designed by Edward Thompson and introduced in 1942, a total of 410 of these versatile locomotives were built. On the right and going through the white gate is the Woodbridge tramway. This served riverside premises and ran parallel to the main line for a short distance.
Copyright John Hart/E. M. Johnson collection
Photographer John Hart

A view of the East Suffolk line north of Woodbridge and showing the tramway on the right. LNER Class D16/3 4-4-0 No. 2557 heads south with a stopping passenger train.
Copyright John Hart/E. M. Johnson collection
Photographer John Hart

"Britannia" Class 7MT 4-6-2 locomotives became a common sight on East Suffolk services in the 1950s. One of the class, No. 70001 *Lord Hurcomb*, is seen here leaving Woodbridge with a London Liverpool Street - Lowestoft/Yarmouth through train. After being made redundant in East Anglia by diesel traction and spending a few years working in the north west, *Lord Hurcomb* was scrapped in August 1966.
Copyright John Hart/E. M. Johnson collection
Photographer John Hart

A Metropolitan-Cammell DMU forming an Ipswich service waits to leave Woodbridge on Wednesday 24th April 1963. At that time most services on the East Suffolk line were DMU operated between Yarmouth South Town, Lowestoft and Ipswich. Hauled summer Saturday trains still ran on the route to London. The hauled Lowestoft Central - Liverpool Street through train left at 7.30am complete with miniature buffet car on weekdays. All trains stopped at Woodbridge.
Courtesy Anglian Rail Archive

Before steam traction was replaced by diesel multiple units, Class J15 0-6-0 No. 65467 of Ipswich shed was often found at work between Aldeburgh and Saxmundham. Here the locomotive leaves Woodbridge with a train for Ipswich in the late 1950s.
Copyright John Hart/E. M. Johnson collection
Photographer John Hart

In 1961, Worlington Golf Links Halt had a weekday service of four trains to Mildenhall, three to Cambridge (two of which ran via Newmarket) and one to Ely. The halt, seen here complete with the steps required for passengers to board or alight from trains, was one mile from Mildenhall and closed in 1962.
Courtesy Anglian Rail Archive

On Saturday 4th May 1940 at Worlingworth we find LNER Class J65 0-6-0 No. 7157 heading a mixed train. These locomotives were ideal for working the various East Anglian minor country routes such as the Mid Suffolk Light Railway. Under the GER, this type of locomotive had been known as the Class E22 with LNER No. 7157 starting life as GER Class E22 No. 157.
This locomotive was withdrawn from service in November 1947 as LNER No. 8212 following a renumbering exercise by the LNER.
HMRS/Eric S. Russell Collection - Courtesy of the LNWR Society

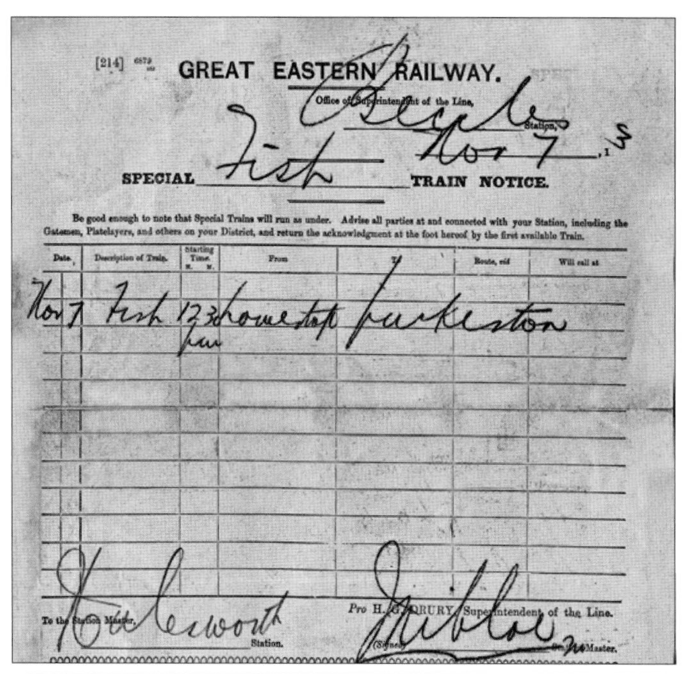

[214] 6879

GREAT EASTERN RAILWAY.

Office of Superintendent of the Line,

Beccles Station,

Nov 7, 13

SPECIAL Fish TRAIN NOTICE.

Be good enough to note that Special Trains will run as under. Advise all parties at and connected with your Station, including the Gatemen, Platelayers, and others on your District, and return the acknowledgment at the foot hereof by the first available Train.

Date.	Description of Train.	Starting Time.	From	To	Route, via	Will call at
Nov 7	Fish	1 23 pm	Lowestoft	Parkeston		

To the Station Master, Halesworth Station.

Pro H. G. DRURY, Superintendent of the Line.

(Signed) Station Master.

Great Eastern Railway

63993

District Engineer's Office, Ipswich Station,

W. G. 174/191

Oct 26/03.

Dear Sir,

AMOUNTS TO BE DEDUCTED FROM WAGES ENTERED ON PAY SHEETS.

Please deduct amounts as shewn on the other side and pay same in to the credit of this Department.

Please note.

Yours truly,

Mr. Skuffham, Station Master, Halesworth

Name.	Grade.	No of Pay Sheet.	Week ending.	Amount to be Deducted.
Smith. G	P'layer	36	23/10/03.	-/9.

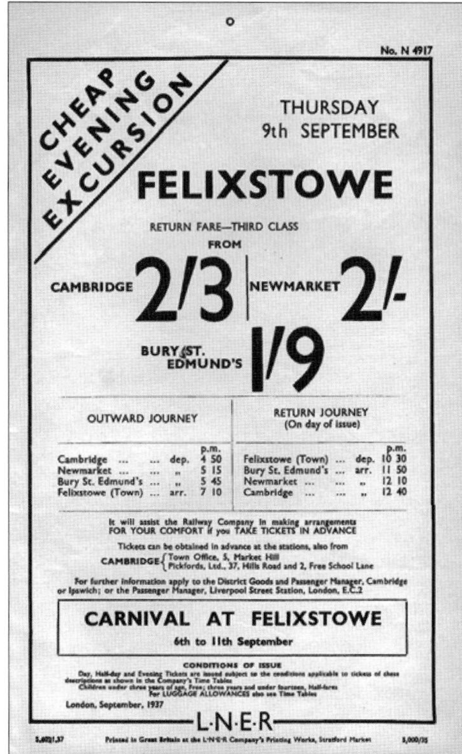

No. N 4917

CHEAP EVENING EXCURSION

THURSDAY 9th SEPTEMBER

FELIXSTOWE

RETURN FARE—THIRD CLASS FROM

CAMBRIDGE 2/3 NEWMARKET 2/-

BURY ST. EDMUND'S 1/9

OUTWARD JOURNEY		p.m.	RETURN JOURNEY (On day of issue)		p.m.
Cambridge	dep.	4 50	Felixstowe (Town)	dep.	10 30
Newmarket	"	5 15	Bury St. Edmund's	arr.	11 50
Bury St. Edmund's	"	5 45	Newmarket	"	12 10
Felixstowe (Town)	arr.	7 10	Cambridge	"	12 40

It will assist the Railway Company in making arrangements FOR YOUR COMFORT if you TAKE TICKETS IN ADVANCE

Tickets can be obtained in advance at the stations, also from

CAMBRIDGE { Town Office, 5, Market Hill / Pickfords, Ltd., 37, Hills Road and 2, Free School Lane

For further information apply to the District Goods and Passenger Manager, Cambridge or Ipswich; or the Passenger Manager, Liverpool Street Station, London, E.C.2

CARNIVAL AT FELIXSTOWE

6th to 11th September

CONDITIONS OF ISSUE

Day, Half-day and Evening Tickets are issued subject to the conditions applicable to tickets of these descriptions as shown in the Company's Time Tables

Children under three years of age, Free; three years and under fourteen, Half-fares

For LUGGAGE ALLOWANCES also see Time Tables

London, September, 1937

L·N·E·R

Printed in Great Britain at the L·N·E·R Company's Printing Works, Stratford Market 5,000/35

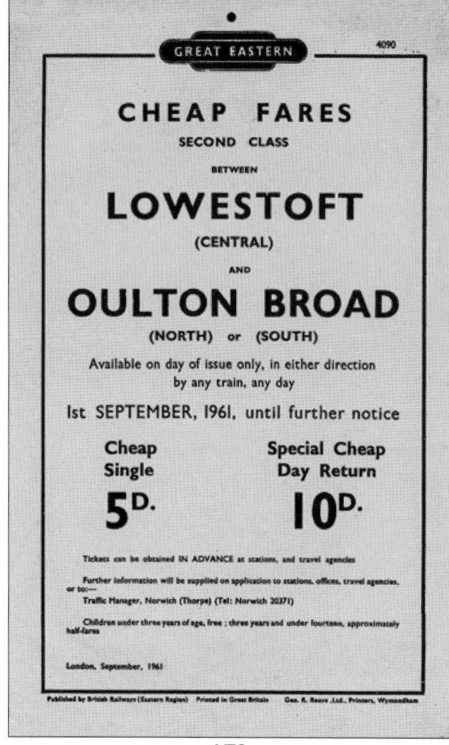

4090

GREAT EASTERN

CHEAP FARES

SECOND CLASS

BETWEEN

LOWESTOFT (CENTRAL)

AND

OULTON BROAD (NORTH) or (SOUTH)

Available on day of issue only, in either direction by any train, any day

1st SEPTEMBER, 1961, until further notice

Cheap Single 5D.

Special Cheap Day Return 10D.

Tickets can be obtained IN ADVANCE at stations, and travel agencies

Further information will be supplied on application to stations, offices, travel agencies, or to:—

Traffic Manager, Norwich (Thorpe) (Tel: Norwich 20371)

Children under three years of age, free ; three years and under fourteen, approximately half-fares

London, September, 1961

Published by British Railways (Eastern Region) Printed in Great Britain Geo. R. Reeve ,Ltd., Printers, Wymondham

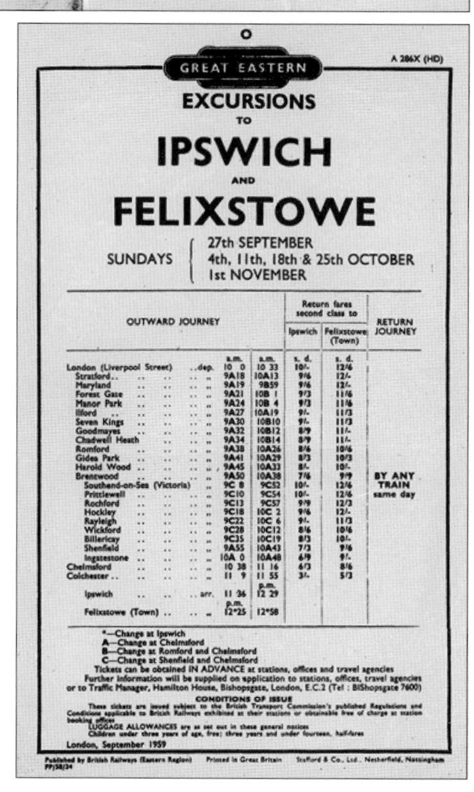

A 286X (HD)

GREAT EASTERN

EXCURSIONS TO

IPSWICH AND FELIXSTOWE

SUNDAYS { 27th SEPTEMBER / 4th, 11th, 18th & 25th OCTOBER / 1st NOVEMBER

OUTWARD JOURNEY				Return fares second class to Ipswich	Return fares second class to Felixstowe (Town)	RETURN JOURNEY
		a.m.	a.m.	s. d.	s. d.	
London (Liverpool Street)	dep.	10 0	10 33	10/-	12/6	
Stratford	"	9A18	10A13	9/6	12/-	
Maryland	"	9A19	9B59	9/6	12/-	
Forest Gate	"	9A21	10B 1	9/3	11/6	
Manor Park	"	9A24	10B 4	9/3	11/6	
Ilford	"	9A27	10A19	9/-	11/3	
Seven Kings	"	9A30	10B10	9/-	11/3	
Goodmayes	"	9A32	10B12	8/9	11/-	
Chadwell Heath	"	9A34	10B14	8/9	11/-	
Romford	"	9A38	10A26	8/6	10/6	
Gidea Park	"	9A41	10A29	8/3	10/3	
Harold Wood	"	9A45	10A33	8/-	10/-	
Brentwood	"	9A50	10A38	7/6	9/9	BY ANY TRAIN same day
Southend-on-Sea (Victoria)	"	9C 8	9C52	10/-	12/6	
Prittlewell	"	9C10	9C54	10/-	12/6	
Rochford	"	9C13	9C57	9/9	12/3	
Hockley	"	9C18	10C 2	9/6	12/-	
Rayleigh	"	9C22	10C 6	9/-	11/3	
Wickford	"	9C28	10C12	8/6	10/6	
Billericay	"	9C35	10C19	8/3	10/-	
Shenfield	"	9A55	10A43	7/3	9/6	
Ingatestone	"	10A 0	10A48	6/9	9/-	
Chelmsford	"	10 38	11 16	6/3	8/6	
Colchester	"	11 9	11 55	3/-	5/3	
			p.m.			
Ipswich	arr.	11 36	12 29			
		p.m.				
Felixstowe (Town)	"	12*25	12*58			

*—Change at Ipswich
A—Change at Chelmsford
B—Change at Romford and Chelmsford
C—Change at Shenfield and Chelmsford

Tickets can be obtained IN ADVANCE at stations, offices and travel agencies

Further information will be supplied on application to stations, offices, travel agencies or to Traffic Manager, Hamilton House, Bishopsgate, London, E.C.2 (Tel : BIShopsgate 7600)

CONDITIONS OF ISSUE

These tickets are issued subject to the British Transport Commission's published Regulations and Conditions applicable to British Railways exhibited at their stations or obtainable free of charge at station booking offices

LUGGAGE ALLOWANCES are as set out in these general notices

Children under three years of age, free; three years and under fourteen, half-fares

London, September 1959

Published by British Railways (Eastern Region) Printed in Great Britain Stafford & Co., Ltd., Netherfield, Nottingham PP/58/34

Opposite

Top - Instructions to the Station Master at Halesworth concerning a special train, and the adjustment of pay for a platelayer.
Bottom - LNER and BR handbills. The LNER example has blue lettering and the BR (GE) examples have green lettering. *Malcolm R. White Collection*

Below and Right - Extracts from the 1958 British Railways leaflet "From the Carriage Window". These originally had dark blue lettering and show distances and the gradient profile of some of the railway lines in the county. *Courtesy Peter Killby*

All documents reduced in size.

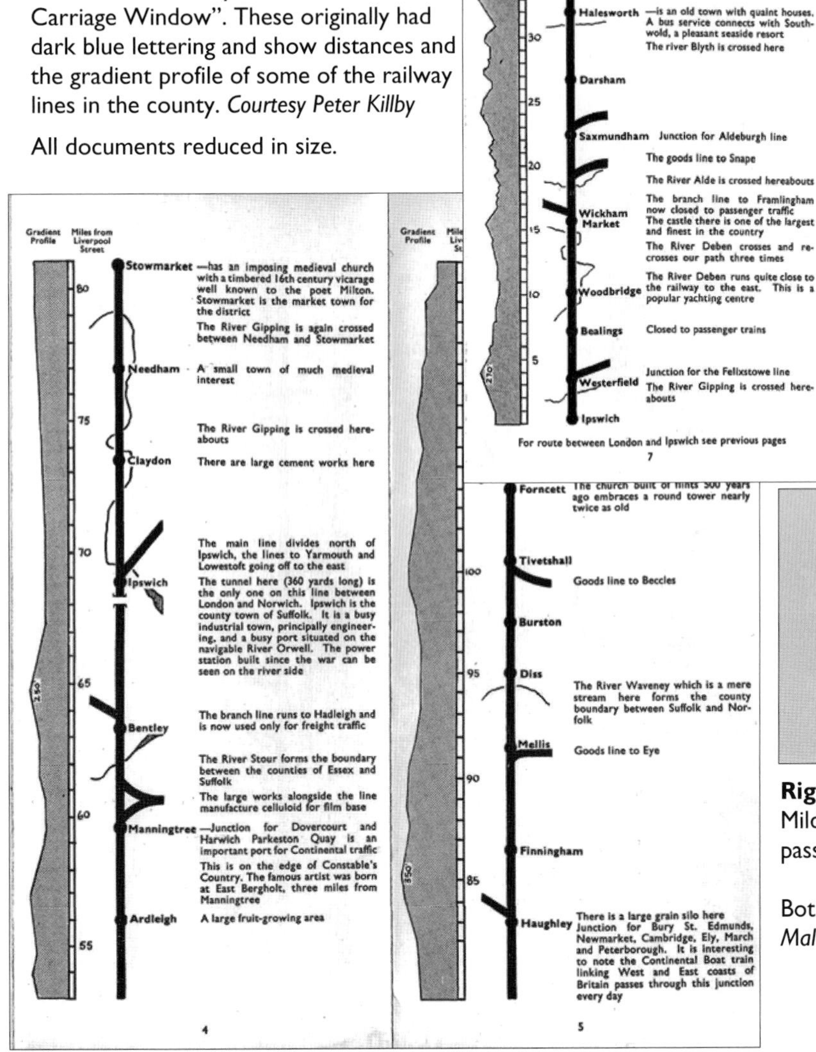

Gradient Profile | Miles from Liverpool Street

Stowmarket —has an imposing medieval church with a timbered 16th century vicarage well known to the poet Milton. Stowmarket is the market town for the district

The River Gipping is again crossed between Needham and Stowmarket

Needham A small town of much medieval interest

The River Gipping is crossed hereabouts

Claydon There are large cement works here

The main line divides north of Ipswich, the lines to Yarmouth and Lowestoft going off to the east

Ipswich The tunnel here (360 yards long) is the only one on this line between London and Norwich. Ipswich is the county town of Suffolk. It is a busy industrial town, principally engineering, and a busy port situated on the navigable River Orwell. The power station built since the war can be seen on the river side

Bentley The branch line runs to Hadleigh and is now used only for freight traffic

The River Stour forms the boundary between the counties of Essex and Suffolk

The large works alongside the line manufacture celluloid for film base

Manningtree —Junction for Dovercourt and Harwich Parkeston Quay is an important port for Continental traffic

This is on the edge of Constable's Country. The famous artist was born at East Bergholt, three miles from Manningtree

Ardleigh A large fruit-growing area

4

Forncett The church built of flints 500 years ago embraces a round tower nearly twice as old

Tivetshall Goods line to Beccles

Burston

Diss The River Waveney which is a mere stream here forms the county boundary between Suffolk and Norfolk

Mellis Goods line to Eye

Finningham

Haughley There is a large grain silo here Junction for Bury St. Edmunds, Newmarket, Cambridge, Ely, March and Peterborough. It is interesting to note the Continental Boat train linking West and East coasts of Britain passes through this junction every day

5

Gradient Profile | Miles from Ipswich

Yarmouth (South Town) Yarmouth is one of the largest seaside resorts in the country with a promenade extending some six miles

Belton & Burgh

St. Olaves The River Waveney is crossed again, taking us back again into Suffolk

Haddiscoe The line from Norwich to Lowestoft is seen here

Aldeby The River Waveney forms the county boundary between Suffolk and Norfolk

Beccles The junction for LOWESTOFT, 8½ miles away with an intermediate station, Oulton Broad South, 6½ miles from Beccles. Lord Nelson's father was married at Beccles church which can be seen from the train

Brampton (Suffolk)

Halesworth —is an old town with quaint houses. A bus service connects with Southwold, a pleasant seaside resort
The river Blyth is crossed here

Darsham

Saxmundham Junction for Aldeburgh line

The goods line to Snape

The River Alde is crossed hereabouts

Wickham Market The branch line to Framlingham now closed to passenger traffic
The castle there is one of the largest and finest in the country

The River Deben crosses and recrosses our path three times

Woodbridge The River Deben runs quite close to the railway to the east. This is a popular yachting centre

Bealings Closed to passenger trains

Westerfield Junction for the Felixstowe line
The River Gipping is crossed hereabouts

Ipswich

For route between London and Ipswich see previous pages

7

TRAIN SPEED TABLES

TIME PER MILE

Time for one mile Mins.	Secs.	Speed m.p.h.	Time for one mile Mins.	Secs.	Speed m.p.h.	Time for one mile Mins.	Secs.	Speed m.p.h.
5	00	12·0	1	5	55·4	0	50	72·0
3	00	20·0	1	4	56·3	0	49	73·5
2	00	30·0	1	3	57·1	0	48	75·0
1	50	32·7	1	2	58·1	0	47	76·6
1	40	36·0	1	1	59·0	0	46	78·3
1	30	40·0	1	0	60·0	0	45	80·0
1	20	45·0	0	59	61·0	0	44	81·8
1	15	48·0	0	58	62·1	0	43	83·7
1	12	50·0	0	57	63·2	0	42	85·7
1	11	50·7	0	56	64·3	0	41	87·8
1	10	51·4	0	55	65·5	0	40	90·0
1	9	52·2	0	54	66·7	0	39	92·3
1	8	52·9	0	53	67·9	0	38	94·7
1	7	53·7	0	52	69·2	0	37	97·3
1	6	54·5	0	51	70·6	0	36	100·0

TIME PER QUARTER MILE

Time for ¼ mile Secs.	Speed m.p.h.	Time for ¼ mile Secs.	Speed m.p.h.	Time for ¼ mile Secs.	Speed m.p.h.
60	15·0	16	56·3	11⅖	78·9
50	18·0	15½	58·1	11⅕	80·4
40	22·5	15	60·0	11	81·8
30	30·0	14½	62·1	10⅘	83·3
25	36·0	14	64·3	10⅗	84·9
22½	40·0	13½	66·7	10⅖	86·5
20	45·0	13	69·2	10⅕	88·2
19½	46·2	12⅘	70·3	10	90·0
19	47·4	12⅗	71·4	9⅘	91·8
18½	48·6	12⅖	72·6	9⅗	93·8
18	50·0	12⅕	73·8	9⅖	95·7
17½	51·4	12	75·0	9⅕	97·8
17	52·9	11⅘	76·3	9	100·0
16½	54·5	11⅗	77·6		

Mile posts and Gradient Boards can be seen on the Down side of the line

Published by British Railways (Eastern Region) PP4101 1958
BR 35159 Printed in Great Britain by Waterlow & Sons Ltd., London and Dunstable

8

FROM THE CARRIAGE WINDOW

the route of

THE EAST ANGLIAN
THE BROADSMAN
THE NORFOLKMAN
THE EASTERLING

London
Ipswich
Norwich **Beccles**
Cromer **Yarmouth**
Sheringham **Lowestoft**

The route diagram included in this folder is intended to interest passengers while on train journeys between London (Liverpool Street) and Ipswich, Norwich, Cromer, Sheringham and Yarmouth

BRITISH RAILWAYS

G. E. R.

Blythburgh

Left - GER luggage label for the Southwold Railway station at Blythburgh. This closed to passengers in April 1929.

Right - GER luggage label for Mildenhall, which closed to passengers in June 1962.

Both labels are reduced in size.
Malcolm R. White Collection

G. E. R.

From ____________________

TO

MILDENHALL

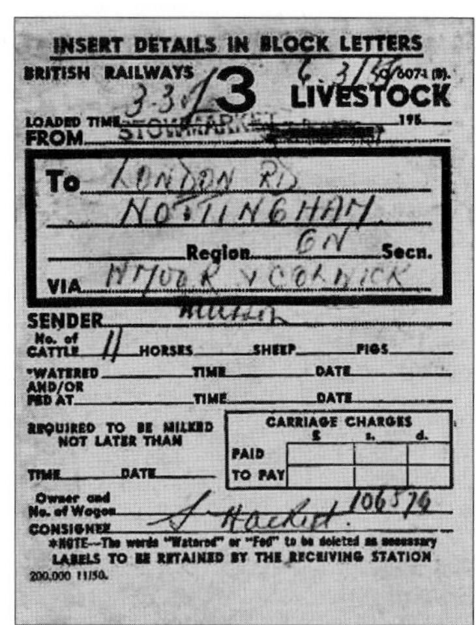
INSERT DETAILS IN BLOCK LETTERS
BRITISH RAILWAYS 3 LIVESTOCK
LOADED FROM STOWMARKET
To LONDON RD NOTTINGHAM
Region GN Secn.
VIA W/MOOR & COLWICK
SENDER
No. of CATTLE 11 HORSES SHEEP PIGS
*WATERED AND/OR FED AT TIME DATE
REQUIRED TO BE MILKED NOT LATER THAN
CARRIAGE CHARGES £ s. d.
PAID
TO PAY
TIME DATE
Owner and No. of Wagon 106576
CONSIGNEE
*NOTE—The words "Watered" or "Fed" to be deleted as necessary
LABELS TO BE RETAINED BY THE RECEIVING STATION
200,000 11/50.

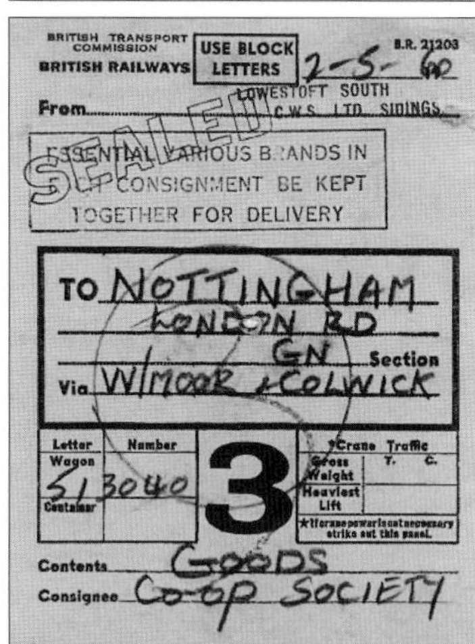
BRITISH TRANSPORT COMMISSION
BRITISH RAILWAYS
USE BLOCK LETTERS
B.R. 21203
2-5-60
From LOWESTOFT SOUTH C.W.S. LTD. SIDINGS
SEALED
ESSENTIAL VARIOUS BRANDS IN CONSIGNMENT BE KEPT TOGETHER FOR DELIVERY
TO NOTTINGHAM LONDON RD
GN Section
Via W/MOOR & COLWICK
Letter Number
Wagon
513040
Container
3
Crane Traffic
Gross Weight T. C.
Heaviest Lift
Contents GOODS
Consignee CO-OP SOCIETY

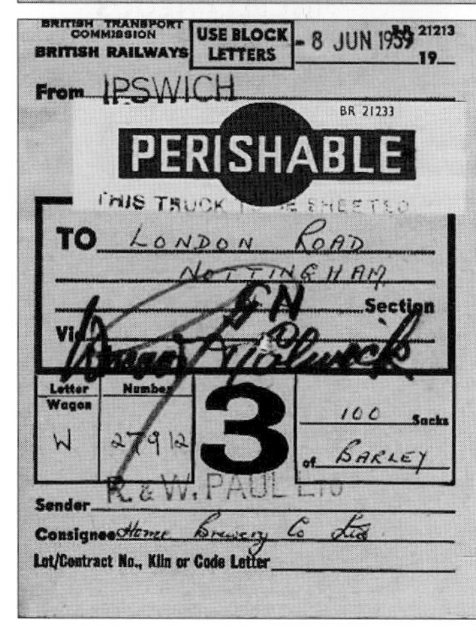
BRITISH TRANSPORT COMMISSION
BRITISH RAILWAYS
USE BLOCK LETTERS
8 JUN 1959
B.R. 21213
From IPSWICH
BR 21233
PERISHABLE
THIS TRUCK TO BE SHEETED
TO LONDON ROAD NOTTINGHAM
GN Section
Letter Number
Wagon
W 27912
3
100 Sacks
of BARLEY
Sender R. & W. PAUL LTD
Consignee
Lot/Contract No., Kiln or Code Letter

LEFT- EXAMPLES OF GOODS SENT BY RAIL FROM SUFFOLK

All three labels are reduced in size and were originally pink in colour with black lettering.

Top - Eleven cattle sent from Stowmarket on 6th March 1957.

Centre - Sealed goods sent from the south Lowestoft factory sidings of the Co-operative Wholesale Society on 2nd May 1960.

Bottom - 100 sacks of barley sent from R. & W. Paul at Ipswich on 8th June 1959. The word "Perishable" is in white on a blue background.

PHOTOGRAPHIC INDEX

MISCELLANEOUS

BOOK DETAILS

Published by Malcolm R. White
Coastal Publications
71 Beeching Drive
Lowestoft
NR32 4TB
First Published June 2010

Printed by Micropress Printers Ltd.
27 Norwich Road
Halesworth
Suffolk
IP19 8BX
ISBN 9780954732370

OTHER TITLES IN THIS UNIQUE SERIES

Maritime Section

		ISBN
DOWN THE HARBOUR 1955-1995	40 years of fishing vessels, owners, the harbour and shipyards at Lowestoft	09532485 0X
A CENTURY OF FISHING	Fishing from Great Yarmouth and Lowestoft 1899-1999	09532485 18
FISHING WITH DIVERSITY	A portrait of the Colne Group of Lowestoft	9780953248520
CROWNIES OF LOWESTOFT	The steam trawler fleet of Consolidated Fisheries	9780953248537
DRIFTING, TRAWLING AND SHIPPING	A portrait of Small & Co. (Lowestoft) Ltd.	9780953248544
THE BOSTON PUTFORD STORY (1)	Fishing and Offshore Support from Great Yarmouth and Lowestoft	9780953248582
HERRINGS, DRIFTERS AND THE PRUNIER TROPHY	Aspects of the vanished herring industry at Yarmouth, Lowestoft and Southwold	9780954732349

Road and Rail Transport Section

THE LOWESTOFT TRAIN	The railway at Lowestoft and scenes on the lines to Norwich, Ipswich and Yarmouth	9780953248568
LOWESTOFT CORPORATION TRANSPORT	Lowestoft Trams, Buses and Bygone Town Scenes	9780953248599
RAILS TO THE COAST	East Anglian Seaside Stations, Sheds and Rail Links-Great Yarmouth and Lowestoft	9780954732301
THE YARMOUTH TRAIN	The railway at Yarmouth and scenes on the lines to Norwich, Ipswich, Melton Constable and Lowestoft	9780954732325
COACHWORK BY EASTERN COACH WORKS	The East Anglian Bus & Coach Builder	9780954732356

Local History Section

GREETINGS FROM LOWESTOFT	A picture book of old postcards and photographs	9780953248551
LOWESTOFT ANTIQUITY	A picture book of once familiar scenes	9780953248575
A SMILE FROM OLD LOWESTOFT	A celebration of bygone scenes, achievements and features	9780954732332
A DIFFERENT LOWESTOFT	Some missing features of a grand old town	9780954732318
CO-OPERATIVE PRIDE AND CAPABILITY	Co-operative Wholesale Society Canning and Preserved Food Factories Lowestoft	9780954732363

Please note that some titles in this popular series are no longer available to purchase new. However copies are held in many local and national libraries and previously owned copies may occasionally be available through dealers and the trade. These books are much sought after and often considered as "collectibles" thereby attracting high prices.

A bygone Suffolk scene (1) - The W. H. Smith bookstall at Lowestoft Central was demolished in 1992 after a period of trading as "Mullanes". A small shop at the station now sells newspapers, sweets and other items. *Courtesy Peter Killby*

A bygone Suffolk scene (2) - Class B12/1 4-6-0 No. 8541 heads a passenger train in the county during the early 1930s. Rebuilt in 1936 to Class B12/3, No. 8541 was scrapped at Stratford in 1957 as No. 61541. *Courtesy Anglian Rail Archive*